JIM SANBORN

ATOMIC TIME

Pure Science and Seduction

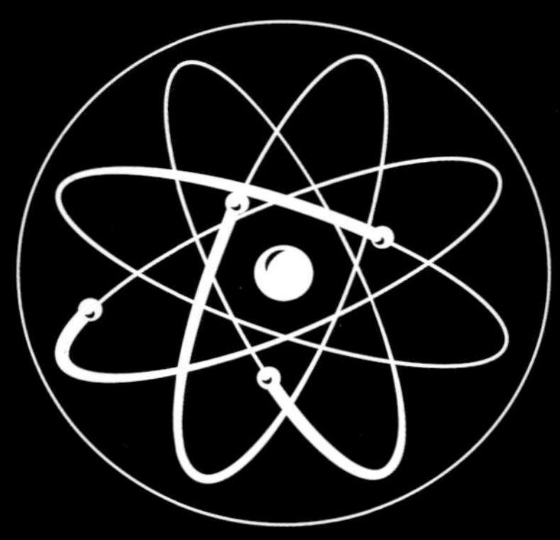

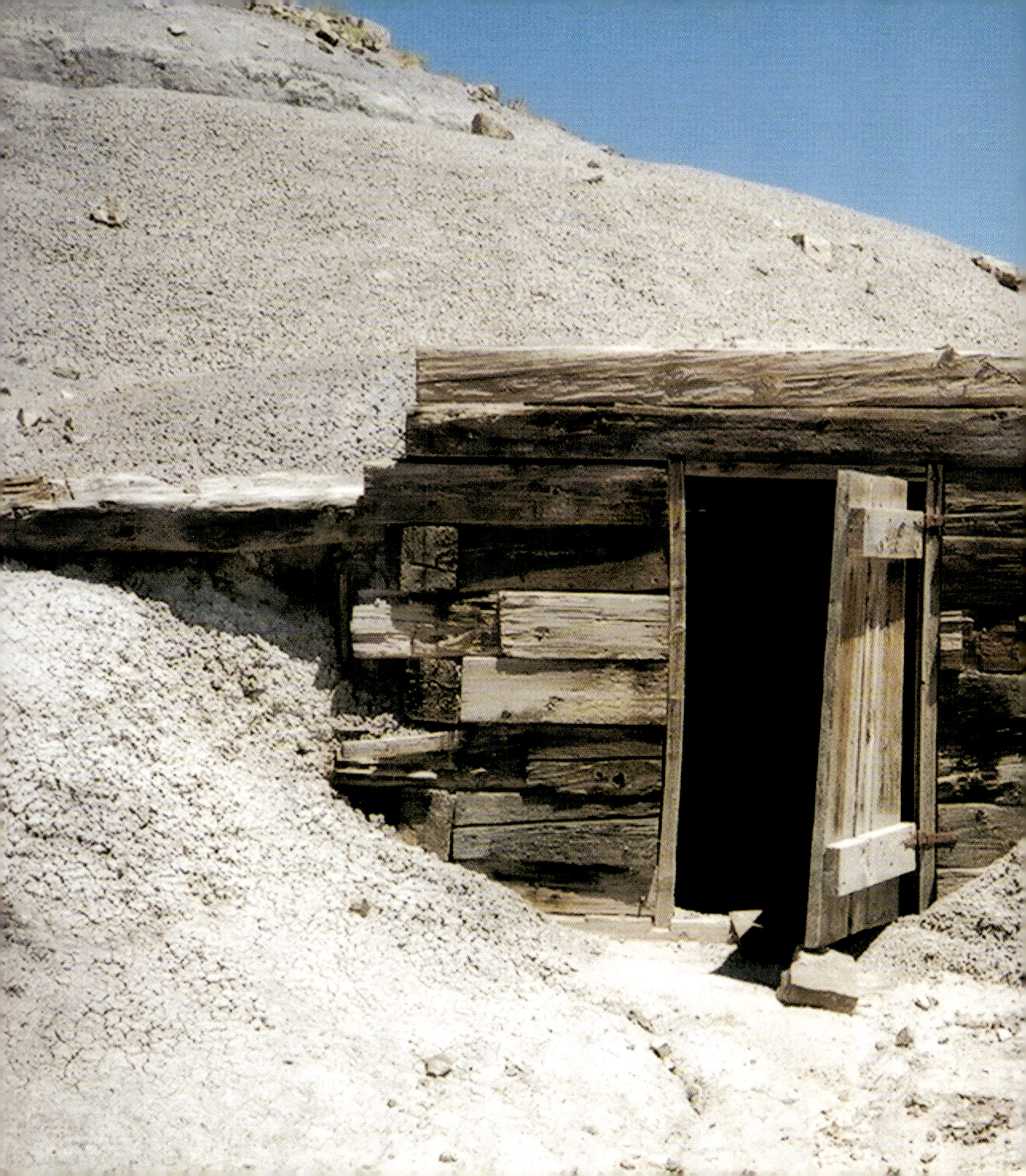

JIM SANBORN

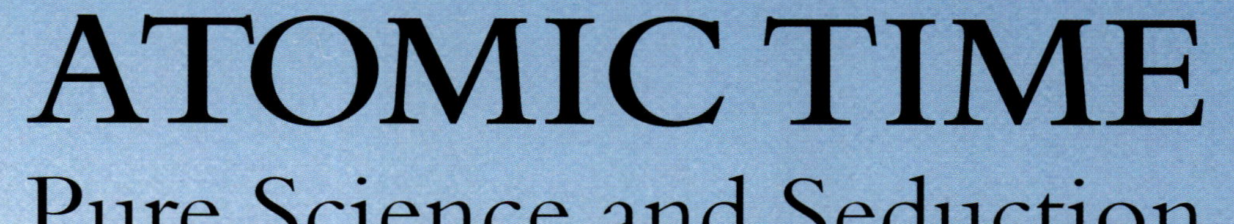

ATOMIC TIME
Pure Science and Seduction

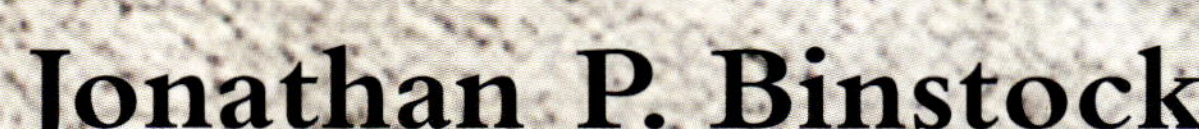

Jonathan P. Binstock

Foreword by
Jacquelyn Days Serwer

With contributions by
Milena Kalinovska
Barbara London
Howard Morland

Corcoran Gallery of Art, Washington, D.C.

Published on the occasion of *Atomic Time: Pure Science and Seduction,* an exhibition of work by Jim Sanborn, organized by Jonathan P. Binstock at the Corcoran Gallery of Art, Washington, D.C., November 1, 2003, to January 26, 2004.

Funding for the exhibition and catalogue is provided by anonymous donors, The President's Exhibition Fund, the Artist-in-Residence Program, initiated by a bequest from Nancy Maloley, and The Andrew W. Mellon Publications Fund at the Corcoran Gallery of Art.

Editor: Janet Wilson

Printed by Bookbuilders, Hong Kong

© 2003 Corcoran Gallery of Art
500 17th Street, N.W.
Washington, D.C. 20006

All rights reserved.

Title page: Uranium mine near Green River, Utah, 2000

Library of Congress Cataloging-in-Publication Data

Binstock, Jonathan P., 1966-
Atomic time : pure science and seduction / author, Jonathan P. Binstock ; foreword by Jacquelyn Days Serwer ; with contributions by Milena Kalinovska, Barbara London, Howard Morland.
p. cm.
Published on the occasion of an exhibition at the Corcoran Gallery of Art, Washington, D.C., Nov. 1, 2003-Jan. 26, 2004.
At head of title: Jim Sanborn.
Includes bibliographical references and index.
ISBN 0-88675-072-5 (alk. paper)
1. Sanborn, Jim, 1945---Exhibitions. 2. Atomic bomb in art--Exhibitions. 3. Installations (Art)--United States--Exhibitions. I. Sanborn, Jim, 1945- II. Corcoran Gallery of Art. III. Title.
N6537.S315A4 2003
709'.2--dc21
2003008435

ISBN 0-88675-072-5

Contents

Foreword

Jacquelyn Days Serwer, Chief Curator, Corcoran Gallery of Art

For generations the Corcoran Gallery of Art has been at the forefront of cutting-edge contemporary art in Washington. William Wilson Corcoran, who founded the institution in 1869, built his collection by acquiring signature works by the most celebrated artists of his time. He envisioned the contents of his museum not only as a source of pleasure for the culture-deprived inhabitants of the capital but also as touchstones for future artists through the institution's collaboration with the Corcoran School of Art (now the Corcoran College of Art+Design). The establishment of the Corcoran Biennial in 1907 reinforced a commitment to the new and daring, one that continues to define the Corcoran's mission today.

Atomic Time: Pure Science and Seduction presents Jim Sanborn's vision of the historic laboratory that proved to be not only the cradle of the atomic bomb but also of the technological age that has so thoroughly defined our lives ever since. His installation, in its beauty, ambiguity, and obsession with authentic detail, aptly reflects the interconnectedness of politics, history, science, and art for many contemporary artists. As the essays in this volume make clear, Sanborn has worked in this complex realm throughout most of his career. From his environmental projects and explorations of invisible natural forces to his commission for the Central Intelligence Agency, in which he investigated the science as well as the art and political context of the age-old practice of cryptography, Sanborn's art has been a point of convergence for the disparate forces that shape contemporary life.

The exhibition could not have come at a more timely moment. In the recent war with Iraq, the United States used an arsenal of high-technology weapons that could not help but amaze and horrify us as well as our enemies. But it seems that no time in recent years has been without a relevant context. When we first began planning the exhibition, during the summer of 2001, tensions were high because of the standoff between two nuclear neighbors, India and Pakistan. Later, the talk focused on North Korea and the imminent reactivation of its nuclear program. Undoubtedly technology, power, and politics will remain vital issues in the conduct of world affairs. Sanborn's exquisite yet ominous installation provides us with the perfect occasion to examine both the beauty of scientific and technological solutions and the perilous applications to which they may lend themselves.

Located in Washington, D.C., a stone's throw from the White House, the Corcoran is well situated to serve as the locus for such discussions, not in the realm of politics but in the dwelling place of the visual arts. Lest the uninitiated assume that Sanborn has created a replica rather than an aesthetic reinterpretation of the laboratory at Los Alamos, New Mexico, he includes his own eloquent time-lapse photographs of uranium ore and mid-twentieth-century clocks with radium dials whose images derive from the same physical properties that made the bomb possible. The photographs are bright blue, just like the color of the air when a burst of radiation escaped during the critical-assembly process used to create the early weapons: beautiful but deadly, hypnotic but fatal. Fortunately, Sanborn's immersive installation gives us the luxury of safely experiencing the conflicting feelings and reactions associated with an environment where such momentous scientific events took place. But this is no ordinary reality. Instead, we are engaged by an artist's vision of the haunted space where the destiny of our planet changed forever.

We are grateful to Jim Sanborn for the many years he has dedicated to this remarkable presentation. We are also mindful of the courage required to undertake and complete a project devoted to a subject that engenders such strong emotional responses. As a way of acknowledging his accomplishment, Sanborn will be the first participant in the Corcoran's new Artist-in-Residence Program. Funds to initiate this collaborative endeavor of the museum and the college of art have come from a generous bequest to the Corcoran's Women's Committee from the estate of Nancy Maloley. This first major gift to support the program is a testament to Nancy's creativity and dedication to the Corcoran Gallery of Art.

As artist-in-residence, Sanborn will share his work with museum audiences and also devote significant time to discussions and studio sessions with students from the Corcoran College of Art+Design. In this way, we advance the cause of contemporary art in Washington for the current as well as the next generation of artists and art lovers.

Acknowledgments

I would first like to thank the residents of Los Alamos, New Mexico, who entrusted me with the treasured objects they had saved for decades. I am also deeply indebted to the residents of Bedrock, Colorado, and Moab, Utah, for their uranium-mining lore, and particularly to the Bureau of Land Management for its lax stewardship of uranium mines in the western United States. My representation of the Trinity device would not have been possible without the tireless scholarship of John Coster-Mullen, the electrical expertise of Doug Crowe, and the infinite moral support of Chuck Hansen and Howard Morland.

Jim Sanborn

This exhibition and the accompanying catalogue represent the efforts of many people, but I would first like to thank those whose generosity has made the project possible. I am deeply grateful for the crucial support of several anonymous donors, The President's Exhibition Fund, the estate of Nancy Maloley for the Artist-in-Residence Program, and The Andrew W. Mellon Publications Fund at the Corcoran Gallery of Art.

From the start, Jacquelyn Days Serwer, chief curator at the Corcoran, was a strong advocate of the project. I continue to be greatly indebted to her for her belief in my ideas and her willingness to stand behind those beliefs. David C. Levy, the Corcoran's president and director, and Michael Roark, the chief financial and administrative officer, had the difficult task of ensuring that the exhibition and catalogue, among the many projects that are always percolating at the Corcoran, would be realized. Their efforts on behalf of the museum's stimulating exhibition program and their support of this exhibition in particular are most appreciated.

I extend special thanks to Milena Kalinovska, Barbara London, and Howard Morland for their contributions to this handsome publication, which illuminate Sanborn's work in sensitive and informed ways and, in the case of Ms. Kalinovska's interview, the career of a brilliant and challenging artist. The catalogue was published with the dedicated assistance and keen oversight of James Trulove of Grayson Publishing in Washington, D.C. Janet Wilson edited the catalogue. I am thankful for her sharp eye and expertise and for playing a key role in yet another Corcoran publication.

A number of my Corcoran colleagues worked directly on this project and deserve to be singled out for the diligence, professionalism, and grace that dependably characterize their efforts: Elizabeth Parr, exhibitions director; Stacey Schmidt, associate curator of contemporary art; Nancy Swallow, registrar; Kate Gibney, director of corporate and foundation relations; Susan Badder, senior curator of education; Christina DePaul, dean of the Corcoran College of Art+Design; Paul Brewer, director of school exhibitions; Steve Brown, senior director of operations and facilities; Clyde Paton, preparator; Dave Jung, assistant preparator; Corey Hixson, art handler; and Sarah Houlihan, curatorial intern. Cheryl Numark and Morriah Amplo of Numark Gallery, Washington, D.C., provided key assistance whenever it was needed.

Finally, I am very grateful to Jim Sanborn, whose vision, resourcefulness, profound intelligence, and perseverance have led him to create the extraordinary works of art explored here. I am humbled by his accomplishments. The depth and importance of this work can only be hinted at in the pages that follow.

Jonathan P. Binstock

Pure Science, Pure Seduction, Pure Art

Critical Assembly and *AtomicTime*

Jonathan P. Binstock

It is self-evident that nothing concerning art is self-evident anymore,
not its inner life, not its relation to the world, not even its right to exist.
—Theodor W. Adorno[1]

While on a trip to White Sands, New Mexico, in 1998 to photograph the desert landscape, Jim Sanborn came across an unassuming academic report called *The Trinity Experiments*. The 102-page booklet documents the experiments that were designed to measure the physical qualities of the first atomic explosion, which took place at what is now called the Trinity National Historic Landmark, near Alamogordo, New Mexico.[2] Featuring numerous reproductions of vintage black-and-white photographs that depict the site and the experimental apparatuses, the booklet struck Sanborn as an arresting record of the dawning of the nuclear era. He was especially captivated by the pictures showing homespun experiments and measuring devices, seemingly held together by simple constructions of wood, nails, string, and duct tape (fig. 1).

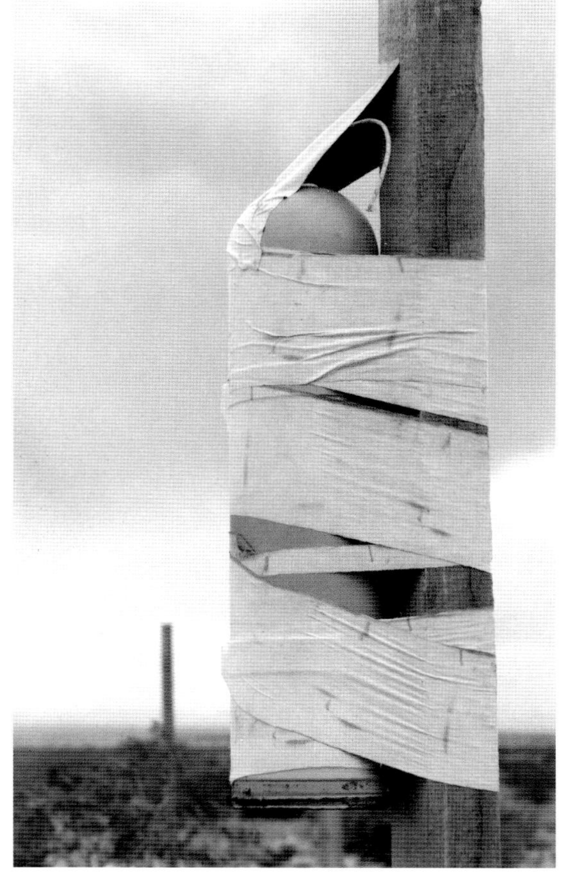

1. Flash bomb, figure 18 from *The Trinity Experiments* by Thomas Merlan

Sanborn's long-standing interest in secrecy and the invisible forces of nature fueled his fast-growing curiosity about the bomb and the history of its development.[3] At the core of the research materials he gathered is a collection of images, those reproduced in *The Trinity Experiments* and others, that highlight a paradoxical characteristic of the scientific work that went into making, detonating, and understanding the effects of the bomb. Here was arguably the most devastating example of scientific invention and applied technology the world has known, yet the machinery used to measure its impact looks like gadgetry that someone's grandfather might have cobbled together in his basement workshop. Other pictures Sanborn found, of a disheveled and even dirty Los Alamos National Laboratory, show mechanical and electronic devices strewn about (fig. 19). Some of it appears, like the machinery in *The Trinity Experiments*, held together by make-do fasteners and other amateur-looking assembly techniques. How could these be depictions of the most advanced nuclear science and experimental research of its day? Sanborn found the incongruities astonishing.

Sanborn's discovery of *The Trinity Experiments* booklet began a five-year investigation into the Manhattan Project (1942–45), the code name given to the U.S. government research project that produced the first atomic bombs. An important aspect of his investigation focused on the ethics of pure scientific research, and how these ethics are compromised by the demand for new technological applications of advanced science. But above all, Sanborn was in search of the aesthetic potential of his investigation, how what he was discovering for himself could form the basis of an expressive art form.

His research led him inexorably to Los Alamos, the town just north of Santa Fe where the government established its laboratory for designing and fabricating atomic bombs. He explored its environs, where he met people, most of them retirees, including physicists, engineers, and firemen, who had worked directly on the Manhattan Project. These individuals contributed personal oral histories to his rapidly expanding knowledge, and they directed him to other sources of information. He met a few people who owned elements of the lab's contents, and one man in particular who had been exhaustively collecting the lab's electronic instruments. All of these people had purchased their collectibles directly from the Los Alamos National Laboratory during the 1960s. Since the 1950s, the lab has opened its doors on weekends and sold old equipment to anyone wishing to buy it. These sales are part of its ongoing effort to liquidate capital investment property thought to be no longer useful.[4] It is easy to understand how a Geiger counter, a device for measuring radiation, manufactured in 1942 could quickly become outdated.

According to the retired scientists, engineers, and their colleagues who collected such things, it is much more difficult to understand why the lab could forsake the historical value of this material. Sanborn had not considered the possibility that these electronic instruments would be accessible to him, let alone that he might be able to acquire examples of them. However, some of the retired collectors, convinced of Sanborn's integrity and the authenticity of his artistic project, sold parts of their holdings to him. He ultimately used this material to make a representation of the lab as it might have existed in the 1940s and 1950s. The machines, electronic instruments, Marchant calculators, and pieces of furniture that he bought, complete with government property numbers identifying them as components of the Los Alamos National Laboratory from the period, are the foundation of his installation, *Critical Assembly* (1998–2003).

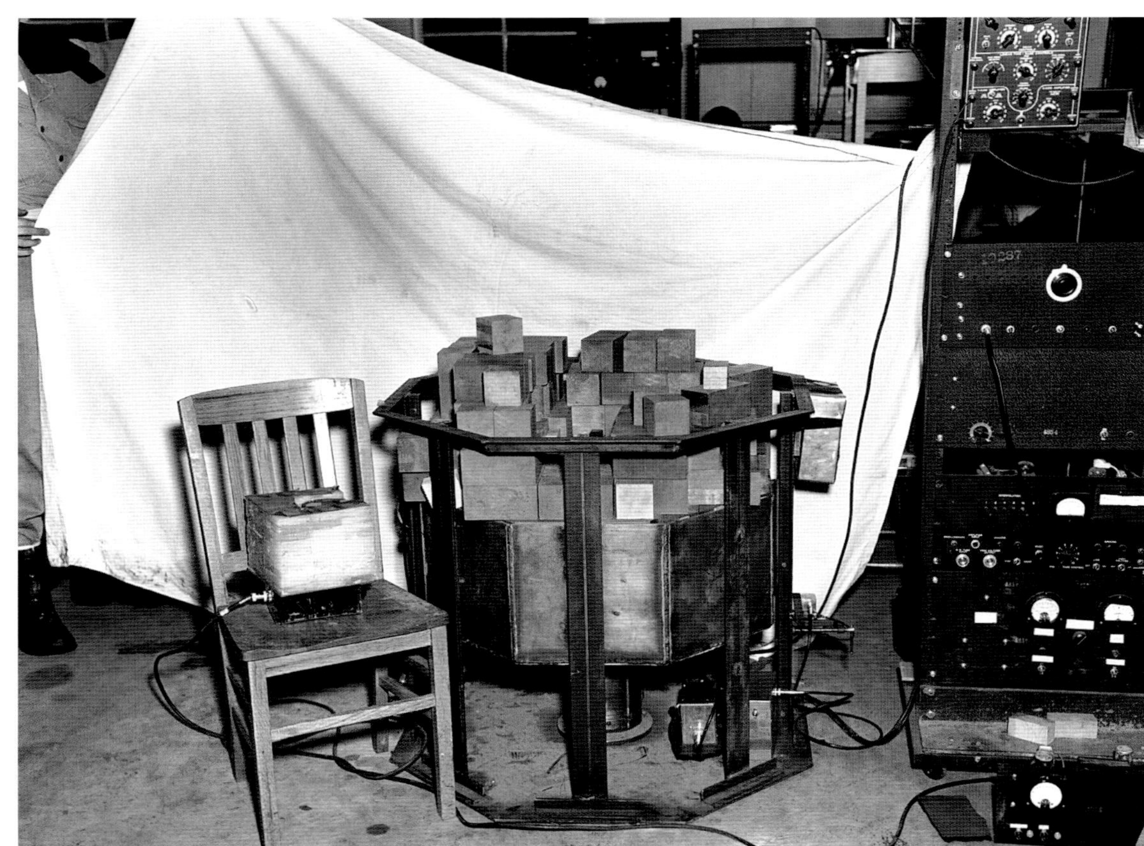

2. Los Alamos National Laboratory
Critical Assembly, c. 1945
Courtesy the Los Alamos National Laboratory

Although *Critical Assembly* includes vintage machinery from the actual lab at Los Alamos, it is, intentionally, not an accurate representation of the historic site. In the first place, very little unclassified information is available to suggest what the lab looked like in its entirety. The Los Alamos laboratory of the 1940s and 1950s occupied, as it does today, most of the land of the town in which it is located. Knowledge of its interior comes to us piecemeal through the aging memories of those who worked there and the few photographs that have been publicly circulated. We have only an assortment of images, for example, of particular stations within the lab, critical assemblies, and snapshots of the bombs in different states. Often a photographer would deliberately obscure expansive vistas of the lab's interior. In one picture, an assistant is shown holding up a white sheet to block views of what lies behind him or an electronic console nearby—a shockingly unsophisticated effort to keep highly classified information secret (fig. 2).

Sanborn's image of the lab is also unlike those depicted in the handed-down photographs because he deliberately altered certain aspects of his representation, either to accentuate the differences between the construction and the real lab or to create an entirely new impression (fig. 6). No one with a reasonable understanding of the historical context would ever confuse the artist's rendering with the actual place. Most strikingly, and in contrast to the documentary photographs, Sanborn's lab is much too clean and neat. Its organization is not based upon functionality or scientific need but rather upon atmospheric effect and the precise demands of his aesthetic.

Like most of Sanborn's art, *Critical Assembly* is exquisitely crafted and scrupulously composed. He has accounted for almost every aspect of the installation and how a person might assimilate the experience: the arrangement and formal interrelations of the various sculptural elements, the source, volume, and tenor of the clicking of the Geiger counters, the placement and intensity of the period light fixtures, the way viewers enter the space and the path of their encounter with the work. Whenever possible, he leaves nothing to chance.

Critical Assembly features a precise replica of the disassembled inner core, also called the physics package, of the first atomic bomb—the Trinity device. The two aluminum hemispheres that constitute the outermost layer of the package, or pusher sphere, are exhibited in different areas of the installation, each commanding its own domain. Within one of the hemispheres the various components of the physics package are nestled inside each other, layer upon layer of rare and radioactive metals, which Sanborn has replaced with nonhazardous counterparts such as brass and bronze (fig. 7). The outer shell is a stunning beach-ball-sized sphere of four-inch-thick aluminum. In a real bomb all of these components would, of course, have a specific function; in his essay for this volume, activist and author Howard Morland describes the various parts and discusses in detail how they would have interacted to generate a nuclear chain reaction. Suffice it to say for the present discussion, there is a formal brilliance to the bomb's composition and, no less, to the overall installation, both in appearance and material. To be sure, no mid-twentieth-century nuclear laboratory, as chaotic as such a lab would have been, ever looked this immaculate or this stunning.

The different critical assemblies, by the force of their visual appeal, similarly beg for some type of formal appreciation. Piled high or low with graphite, lead, or paraffin bricks, they form highly composed sculptural assemblages, each with a distinctive material sensibility. The graphite is lustrous and velvety, with an almost powdery surface that would stain a finger if touched (fig. 10). The lead is dense, heavy, and poisonous—the metal used to make bullets, shaped into brick bullion (fig. 17). A period ceiling lamp illuminating one paraffin critical assembly from above causes the waxy white construction to glow from within (fig. 12). Were this assembly functional, a person might manipulate the bricks of the radiant castlelike structure to slow down the neutrons, to "tickle the dragon's tail," as Morland writes, make music on the Geiger counters, and increase the likelihood that a given neutron would penetrate the nucleus of an atom and cause a chain reaction. From the implied scientific principles to the pure visual attributes, beauty abounds in Sanborn's installation—challenging, potentially hazardous, antagonistic beauty.

There is nothing easy about the installation's appeal, the complexity of which is burdened by a solemn ethical dilemma. While aspects of the installation may dazzle, the work as a whole is unmistakably terrible in its implications. *Critical Assembly* seduces just as it threatens. It invites a person to gaze in wonder at the ingenuity represented and the power implied, just as it bespeaks the horror of some of the twentieth century's most violent acts. There is an urge to touch the various components of the installation despite the menace of the clicking Geiger counters and the oscilloscopes that warn of dangers present.

As a historical tableau, the power of *Critical Assembly* cannot be denied. It is likely to invite passionate responses of all kinds. Some may abhor the allusion to massive human destruction and criticize the installation as a glorification of the bomb, a symbol of the misuse of power. Others may appreciate how the work revisits ongoing unresolved debates about nuclear power, nuclear armament, and weapons research, seeing it as an opportunity to expand on these debates in a new philosophical context. And still others may view it as an example of U.S. intellectual might, resourcefulness, and visionary thinking, a means for pacifying potential threats and achieving world peace. Indeed, some people may be so overcome by the work's topicality that they will be unable to see beyond the ethical questions. They will mistakenly view the work as a historical display, akin to a history museum's diorama, an opportunity to suspend belief and revisit a past time and place. They will miss the work's artistic value entirely.

Coming to grips with *Critical Assembly*'s power and importance as art is a difficult and, I would suggest, anxiety-ridden task, in part because the work is so menacing, so overwhelmingly horrific in its allusions. The challenge it poses derives from two fundamental and competing sources, the historical and the aesthetic. The historical involves ethical issues that inform the practice of pure scientific research; the aesthetic, to which this essay will turn later in greater depth, relates to the perennial debate over what contemporary art can be.

The work's pretense of historical accuracy begins with its collection of actual lab components and filters down to the last details. It finds its fullest realization in the model of the physics package. Extensive research determined most of the dimensions of the various parts that compose the bomb's gadgetry, including the size of the urchin initiator at the core of the physics package and the pusher sphere. The smallest machined forms fit together precisely and snugly inside their

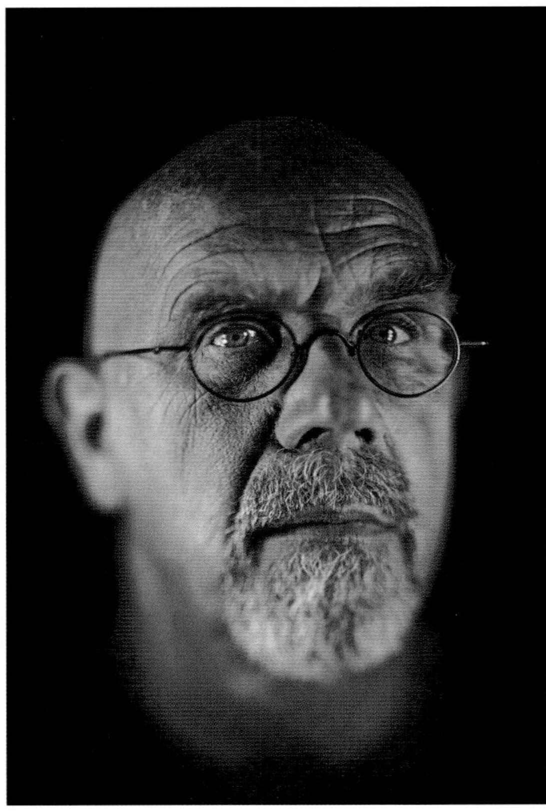
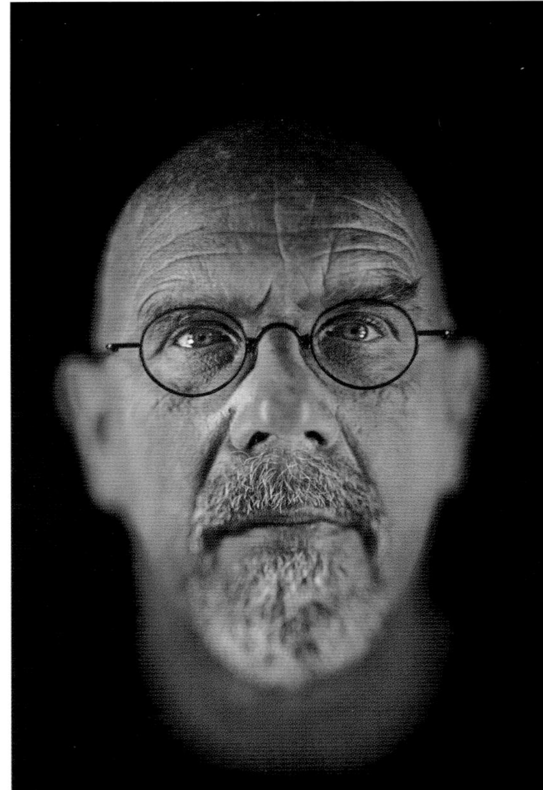
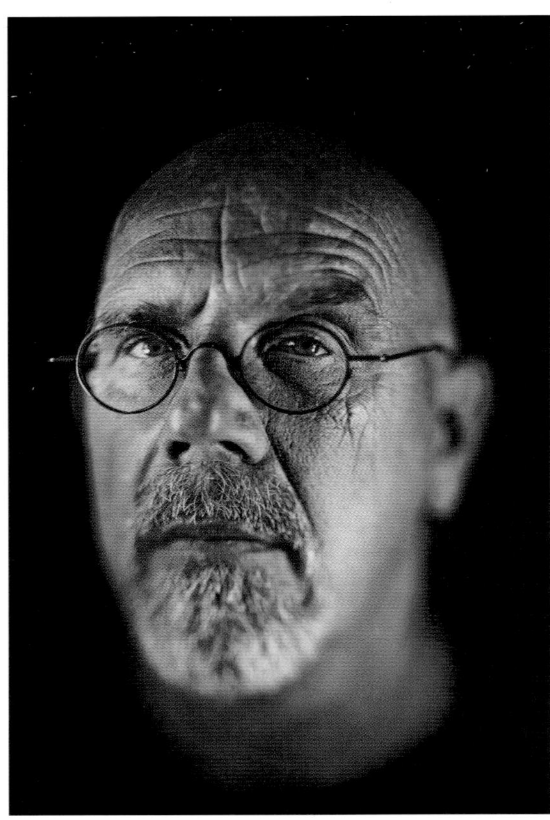

3. Chuck Close
Self-Portrait, 2000
Three daguerreotypes
8 1/2 x 6 1/2" each
Gift of the Women's Committee of the Corcoran Gallery of Art, 2001

proper locations, just as the parts would in an actual bomb. It is in the minutiae that the immensity of the subject is revealed.

This aura of authenticity prompts viewers to address issues that historians, philosophers of science, and scientists themselves have struggled with for decades. Preeminent among them is the problematic relationship between pure scientific research and the technological applications of that research. On the one hand, *Critical Assembly* depicts the laboratory environment where scientists once worked to advance knowledge about the physical world. As Hans Bethe, head of the Theoretical Physics Division of the Manhattan Project, once said, "It is not possible to be a scientist unless you believe that it is good to learn … unless you think that it is of the highest value to share your knowledge, to share it with everyone interested."[5] The Manhattan Project scientists who worked to harness the natural latent power of uranium ore—a rock mined from the earth like coal but capable of yielding as much as three million times the energy of coal—were engaged in this kind of pure scientific research. The direct result of their work was the onset of the nuclear era. The incidental results are many and arguably no less extraordinary—the network of electronics, semiconductors, and computers that developed out of the Manhattan Project and which today constitute the fabric of everyday life. Whether one chooses to describe the overall outcome of the Manhattan Project as mainly good or bad, what originally fueled it, financially and ideologically, was a politically defined national need for a superweapon to defeat enemies of the United States in World War II.

Critical Assembly evokes the ethical dilemma at the heart of pure science's relationship to applied technology by representing a monumental moment in the development of that dilemma. The installation demonstrates how the elegance and beauty of the tools and concepts of atomic science provided a seductive environment in which the scientists at Los Alamos, propelled by the juggernaut of discovery, found themselves at a major ethical crossroads. Many visitors to the exhibition will sense this dilemma, not because they are experts in the history or philosophy of science but rather because Sanborn is able to communicate both the seductive appeal and the danger of atomic research.

Sanborn's challenge in producing *Critical Assembly* was to create an environment in which viewers could understand the allure of atomic science without having to understand its principles. His

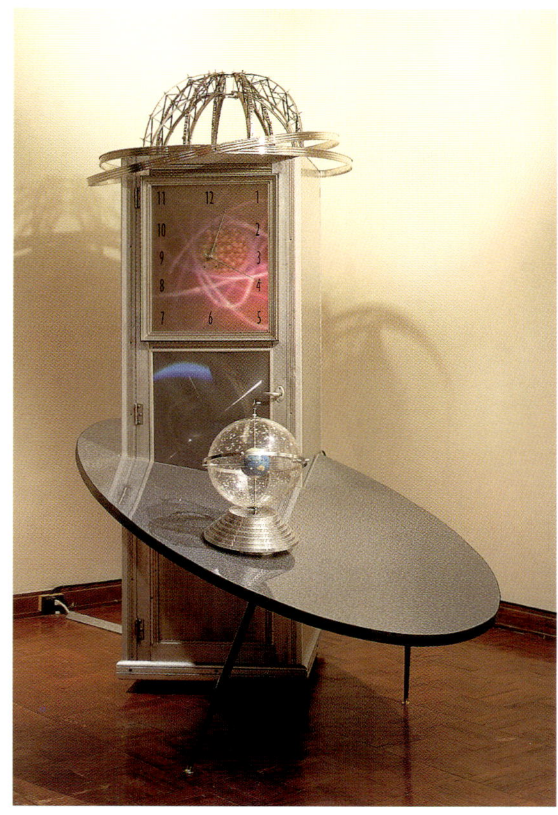

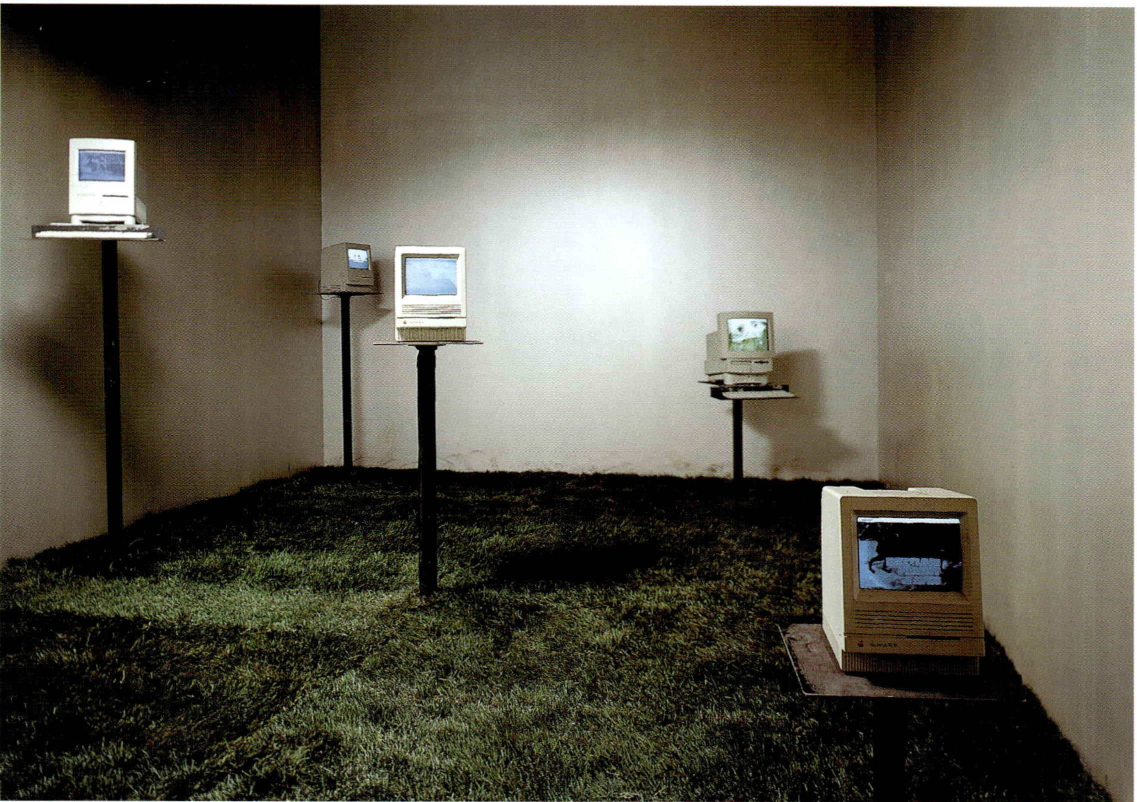

4. Ken Feingold
Childhood/Hot & Cold Wars
(The Appearance of Nature), 1993
Aluminum, glass, plastic, videodiscs, computers, and electronics
100 x 100 x 48"
Courtesy Postmasters Gallery, New York

5. Leah Gilliam
Apeshit v3, 2001
Steel computer stands, live sod, Macintosh computers, digital audio, and computer video
Dimensions variable
Installation view from the exhibition *Bitstreams*, Whitney Museum of American Art, New York
Courtesy the artist

primary means for achieving this effect were the same as those available to all artists: vision and resourcefulness. He objectifies the beauty of atomic science through a commitment to historical accuracy—to the extent that such accuracy is both possible and desirable—and through craft and the skillful manipulation of form, surface, and environment. The striking, jewel-like gleam of his model of the physics package is not only reflective of the actual device but also symbolic of the elegance of the atomic principles underlying the structures. Seduction and threat are the expressive content that enables visitors to sense, albeit metaphorically, the ethical dilemma faced by scientists as they pursued well-designed or, in the parlance of the scientists, "sweet" solutions to their ominous tasks.

By using historical material as the basis for an aesthetic form, *Critical Assembly* makes an important contribution to art's long-standing dialogue with science and technology and to debates about what counts as art. For most of their histories, art and science have been directly linked and, at times, even difficult to distinguish from each other. According to philosopher David C. Graves, not until the mid-eighteenth century did the two go in opposite directions, science toward the rational, art toward the expressive.[6] Since that time, artists have maintained a relationship with science and technology in at least three ways. First, subjects related to science and technology can be represented in two or three dimensions, for example, a medical procedure, as Thomas Eakins did, or a spark plug, as Francis Picabia did. Second, applied technologies can be employed in the service of artistic production, such as a camera obscura to make drawings or a Polaroid camera to make photographs. And third, advanced scientific concepts and technological media can be used in ways that question their original applications and, correspondingly, the boundaries of accepted art forms. Consider, for example, the video artists of the 1960s or the Internet artists of the 1990s, whose use of so-called new media caused opportune reevaluations of the parameters of contemporary art.

Sanborn's *Critical Assembly* exemplifies the first of the aforementioned examples, but with a twist. It is a representation of science and technology in an archaeological context. Sanborn is the artist as engineer—a lineage that includes the machine aesthetics of László Moholy-Nagy, Jean Tinguely, and Alexander Calder, among many others—exhibiting the dinosaur of nuclear labs and weapons, advanced technology from a bygone era.

According to writer, curator, and professor Erkki Huhtamo, archaeological approaches to art media preceded the 1990s, but it was during this decade that such approaches emerged as a wider concern.[7] This can be seen in the recent work of Chuck Close, who has turned to the daguerreotype, one of the oldest photographic processes, to make his portraits (fig. 3). A few other notable artists, such as Ken Feingold and Leah Gilliam, employ actual examples of outmoded technological apparatuses as sculptural elements—zoetropes, kinetoscopes, stereoscopes, household appliances, vintage television sets, obsolete computers and their displays—to explore nostalgia or the consequences of a disposable technology, the flip side of a consumer culture that is constantly advancing (figs. 4 and 5).[8] Sanborn extends this research in singular terms by reconstructing a seminal moment in the history of advanced technology. He uses old equipment not only in the service of new ideas but also to evoke its originally intended application.

In the tradition of the *bricoleur,* Sanborn is a master arranger of found objects. Like Marcel Duchamp, who, in 1913, recontextualized ordinary objects and called them readymades, or the contemporary artists Ann Hamilton and Tom Sachs, he is as much a maker of art installations, an exhibition designer, as he is a maker of art objects.[9] To this end, he has augmented his collection of original lab devices with additional hardware, assembled parts, and furniture that he fabricated to match the vintage examples he had acquired, effectively blurring the distinction between the historical and the created.

A particularly telling example is the stool that populates the installation, which the artist first saw in a photograph of the actual lab (figs. 6 and 19). According to Sanborn, the scientists favored this particular piece of furniture because it resembles a thermonuclear explosion. The seat suggests the apex of a mushroom-shaped cloud shooting up through a ring of dust and debris. After many years of searching the country's flea markets and garage sales, he found only one, in a Georgetown bazaar not far from his home. For the installation he fabricated another three out of plywood—theatrical props that would certainly collapse under a person's weight.[10]

Another example is Sanborn's discovery, in the backyard of a retired Los Alamos laboratory employee, of a forged aluminum blank that was designed to fit into a lathe for machining a pusher sphere. The employee had been using it as a makeshift birdbath. Sanborn purchased several of the blanks and fashioned from them the intended spheres, whose dimensions, he discovered through his research, were exactly the same as those of the Trinity bomb's pusher sphere. This pusher sphere, an accurate replica, is the one presented in the installation.

The stool and the pusher sphere reveal different aspects of the unique confluence of history and aesthetics that characterizes *Critical Assembly*. Sanborn features the stool because it shows that the scientists were perhaps as appreciative of the given object's look as they were of its functionality. Some aspects of the lab are potentially operational, while much of it only implies functionality. Such is the context for interpreting Sanborn's installation, in which science and aesthetics are virtually indistinguishable. In this regard, the stool—what it is and does, and how it simultaneously represents something else—is emblematic of the work's metaphorical operations in general. The overall effect, a finely rendered historical illusion, is the bedrock of its aesthetic charge.

The pusher sphere of the physics package manifests another facet of the science-history-art matrix. However convincing as a replica, it is a representation and, in the end, inevitably historically inaccurate. Sanborn makes it gleam because, as reported in firsthand accounts, the original sphere also gleamed. But the artist was accurate only to the extent that it was possible and, no less important, desirable. The largest of the paraffin assemblies is, in fact, larger than the original construction on which it is based because, as Sanborn has said, he prefers it that way—for purely visual reasons (fig. 12). For every on-point accurate replication there is an alteration, embellishment, or approximation. Driven in part by a desire for historical accuracy, Sanborn ultimately portrayed the lab in terms of his own aesthetic light.

The complexity of Sanborn's approach to historical accuracy, truth to objects and materials, and artifice is further highlighted in the series of photographs, *Atomic Time* (2001–2), that he created while working on the installation. The series consists of two types of images: autoradiographs of small samples of uranium ore and time-lapse photographs of radium-dial alarm clocks. Sanborn made the autoradiographs by placing uranium on still-sealed, ready-load 4x5-inch film packs and allowing the ore to photograph itself. The tonality of the images' faceted forms is brightest where the uranium was most radioactively potent or where the ore touched the film. The images range from abstractions with sharp contrasts and razorlike edges to allover, sweepingly radiant designs, and no two are alike.

In effect, the autoradiographs are straight portraits of the internal formal character of the uranium samples and, more indirectly, portraits of the mines from which they came. The radium-dial alarm clocks represent the other end of the continuum—documents of manufactured goods, radiation commodified for a consumer culture. Straightforward to a point, both types of representation are distinguished by an intense blue color that resembles the true color of radioactivity. This hue, similar to cobalt blue, recalls the glowing atmosphere surrounding intensely radioactive materials. The effect is called Cherenkov radiation, named after the Russian physicist Pavel Cherenkov, who discovered it while experimenting with gamma rays in 1934. Sanborn achieved this look of material truth through his choice of photographic film, paper, and refinements of his working process. It is, at least in part, this color, arrived at laboriously through months of trial and error, that gives the pictures their heavy conceptual weight.

The overall effect of Sanborn's unique brew of historical accuracy and aesthetic license, particularly in the installation, may seem radically uncanny to many viewers, like an eccentric, decades-old vision of the future. Popular culture and the visual forms that often mediate our relationship to the past exert a powerful influence on *Critical Assembly*. The pusher sphere may look more like some sort of futuristic metallic chamber, perhaps a spherical space pod from a science-fiction film, than a drab bombshell. The effect is at least theatrical. And if it seems a bit Hollywood, it is not because Sanborn has embellished the bomb in any way but, rather, it is because of who we are and the culture in which we live.

Thick black cables winding their way around the floor conduct no electricity and serve no practical purpose other than to entangle visitors in an expressive web that threatens to trip them up should they not pay close attention. As one searches the dimly lit confines of the lab for a sense of what it contains, lights on the electronic instruments glow, and the sound of Geiger counters and the images on oscilloscopes detect radioactive material. There is an air of danger and mystery, as if we are interlopers in the confidential arena of government-sponsored research. *Critical Assembly* creates the sensation that the artist has pulled back the veil of secrecy that has shrouded the Los Alamos National Laboratory since its founding. However, this feeling is more the installation's conceit than its actual function. *Critical Assembly* does not reveal classified information. Rather, it is a physical translation of the many textual and photographic descriptions that are readily available in books and on the Internet. If the installation has the air of something secret and prohibited, it is because secrecy is its expressive content, the consequence of Sanborn's inimitable style.

Critical Assembly is a representation of the primal scene, as it were, of the nuclear era, with all of the drama and impact that such a scene might entail. It is simultaneously a symbol of astonishing human achievement and an act of latent yet profound violence, stimulating a dialogue about the allure of pure science and the ethical dilemmas atomic researchers have faced for decades.

During the past twenty years the increasing availability of sophisticated scientific information in scholarly journals and on the Internet has created another type of seductive environment. Previously classified information has turned up unclassified in a variety of ways. The U.S. Freedom of Information Act offers a halting wellspring of previously classified information, as did the informational wave created by the collapse of the Soviet Union. In the past few years huge volumes of this material have become available on the Internet. The release of much of this historical information is often at odds with the mandates of U.S. government agencies responsible for concealing information related to national security. Despite this conflict, the decision to release classified information is often arrived at politically. This installation draws our attention to the paradoxical conflict between government efforts to conceal formerly classified information and the political necessity to make it available. Moreover, it suggests one way individuals in a democratic society may become aware of past, formerly secretive government initiatives and how this information can serve as the basis for an expressive art form.

Art's relationship to politics assumes new meaning in the context of this installation, as does art's relationship to history and science. *Critical Assembly* blurs all of these distinctions. It represents both a contribution to these dialogues and a new interpretation of them. Theoretically it may seem that a chasm separates the aspects of the installation that are objective truths from those that are subjective features. In the context of the artistic experience these differences are indistinguishable. Here, science is a metaphor for art, the scientist for the artist, and the laboratory for the artist's studio. One does not enter the installation to revisit the past or to surrender belief and become immersed in verisimilitude. Rather, one enters the installation to understand what it might reveal about humanity, the drive for knowledge, and the use of power. *Critical Assembly* is an event, a way to affect how people see the world—the past, present, and future—based on the transcendent order of aesthetic principles.

NOTES

1. Theodor W. Adorno, *Aesthetic Theory* (Minneapolis: University of Minnesota Press, 1997), 1.

2. Thomas Merlan, *The Trinity Experiments*, report prepared by Human Systems Research, Inc., for White Sands Missile Range, New Mexico (Tularosa, N.M.: Human Systems Research, Inc., 1997), 1.

3. In an interview for this catalogue with curator Milena Kalinovska, Sanborn discusses the trajectory of his career and the development of his interest in secrecy and invisible forces, among many other related topics.

4. The practice continued for decades but may have halted indefinitely owing to the events of 9/11.

5. Bethe, quoted in Silvan S. Schweber, *In the Shadow of the Bomb: Bethe, Oppenheimer, and the Moral Responsibility of the Scientist* (Princeton, N.J.: Princeton University Press, 2000), 18.

6. David C. Graves, "Art as a Rational Activity," *Journal of Aesthetic Education* 35, no. 4 (Winter 2002): 1.

7. Erkki Huhtamo, "Time Traveling in the Gallery: An Archeological Approach in Media Art," in *Immersed in Technology: Art and Virtual Environments*, edited by Mary Anne Moser with Douglas MacLeod (Cambridge, Mass.: MIT Press, 1996), 233–34.

8. Ibid., 233. The list of technology examples is Huhtamo's.

9. See Sheldon Nodelman, "Duchamp I: Disguise and Display," *Art in America* 91, no. 3 (March 2003): 57–62, 131–32; and the limited-edition catalogue for the exhibition *American Bricolage*, organized by Tom Sachs and David Leiber for Sperone Westwater Gallery, New York, November 2–December 22, 2000.

10. The same can largely be said about other elements of the installation. For example, Sanborn cast the paraffin blocks himself, and many of the lead bricks are actually wood wrapped in a lead sheath. Because of their weight, it would have been impractical to use only actual lead blocks. The light fixtures that illuminate the room and help create the menacing mood were, like the stools, found in the resale marketplace and made by the artist.

Critical Assembly

6. *Laboratory Environment for the Assembly of the Trinity Device, c. 1945*
Aluminum, brass, gold-, silver-, and nickel-plated brass, lead, stainless steel, boron-impregnated plastic, detector probes, Geiger-Muller (G-M) counters, simulated hydraulic lifts, graphite, wire, and sound
12 x 35 x 25', dimensions variable

All works are by Jim Sanborn, 1998–2003, and are shown installed in his studio. Courtesy the artist and Numark Gallery, Washington, D.C.

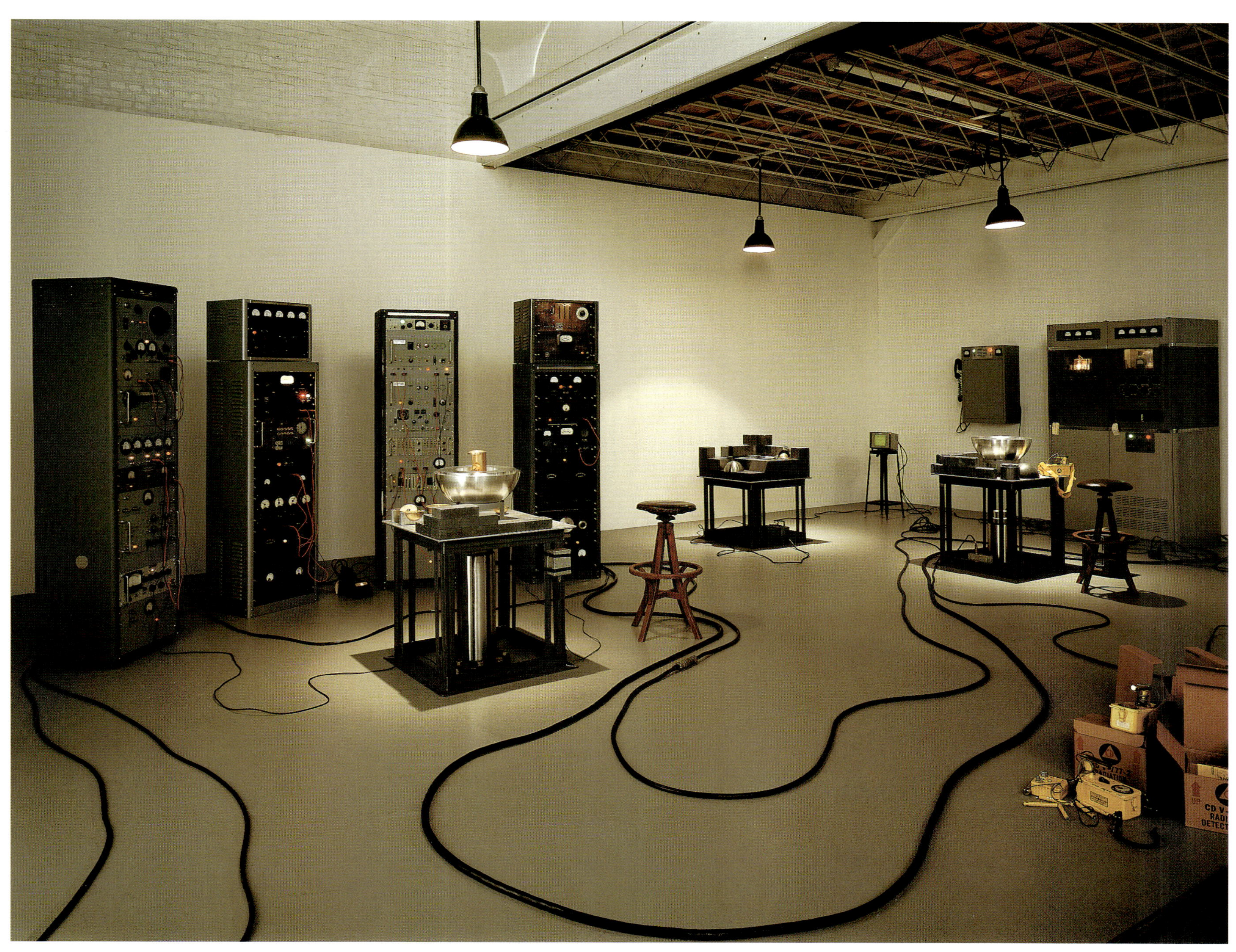

7. *Bottom Half of the Disassembled Physics Package of the Trinity Device*
Aluminum, brass, gold- and silver-plated brass, lead, stainless steel, boron-impregnated plastic, simulated hydraulic lift, alpha detector, graphite, and wire
36 x 48 x 36"

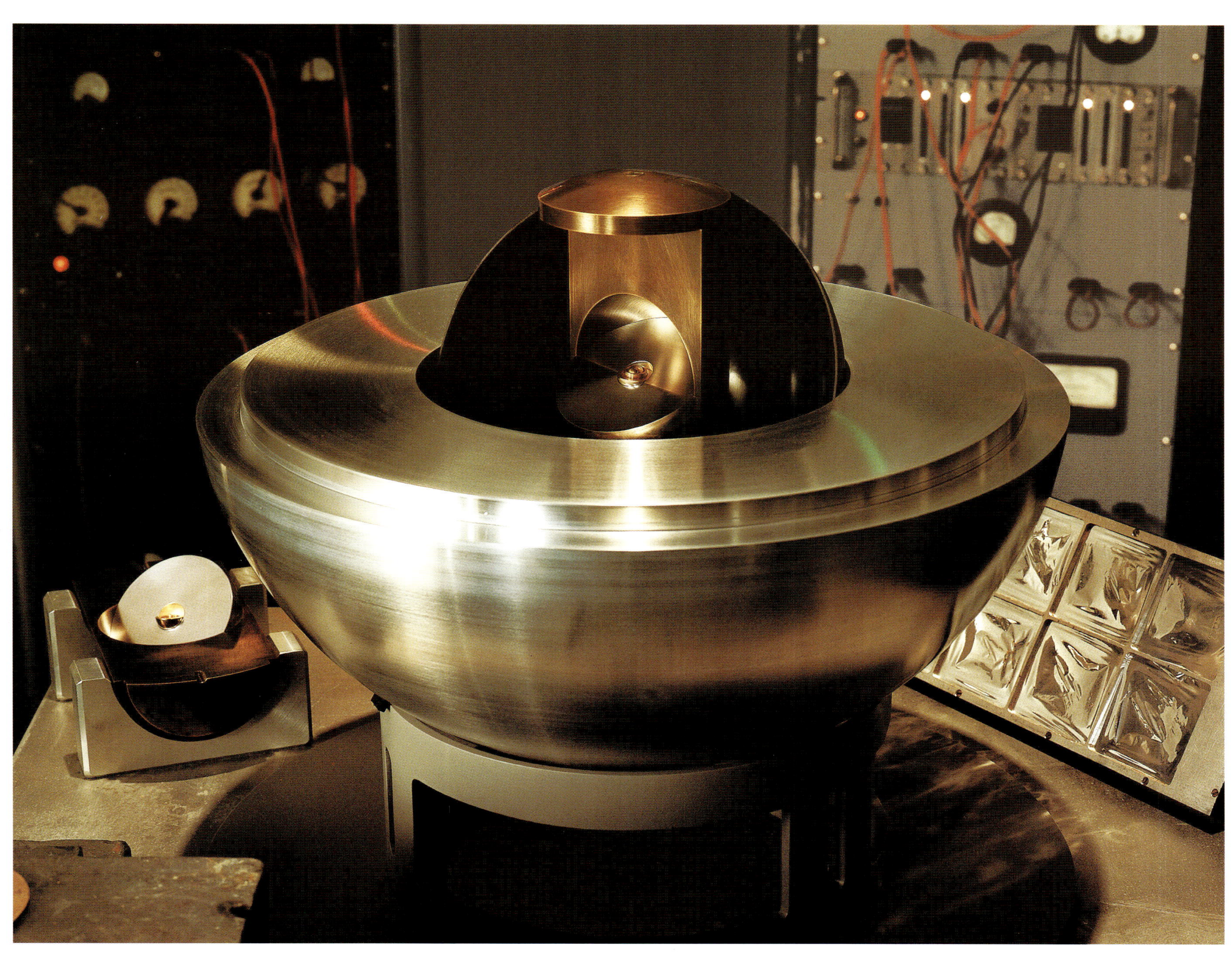

8. *Inverted Top Half of the Disassembled Physics Package of the Trinity Device*
Aluminum, brass, lead, stainless steel, boron-impregnated plastic, G-M counter, simulated hydraulic lift, graphite, and wire
36 x 48 x 36"

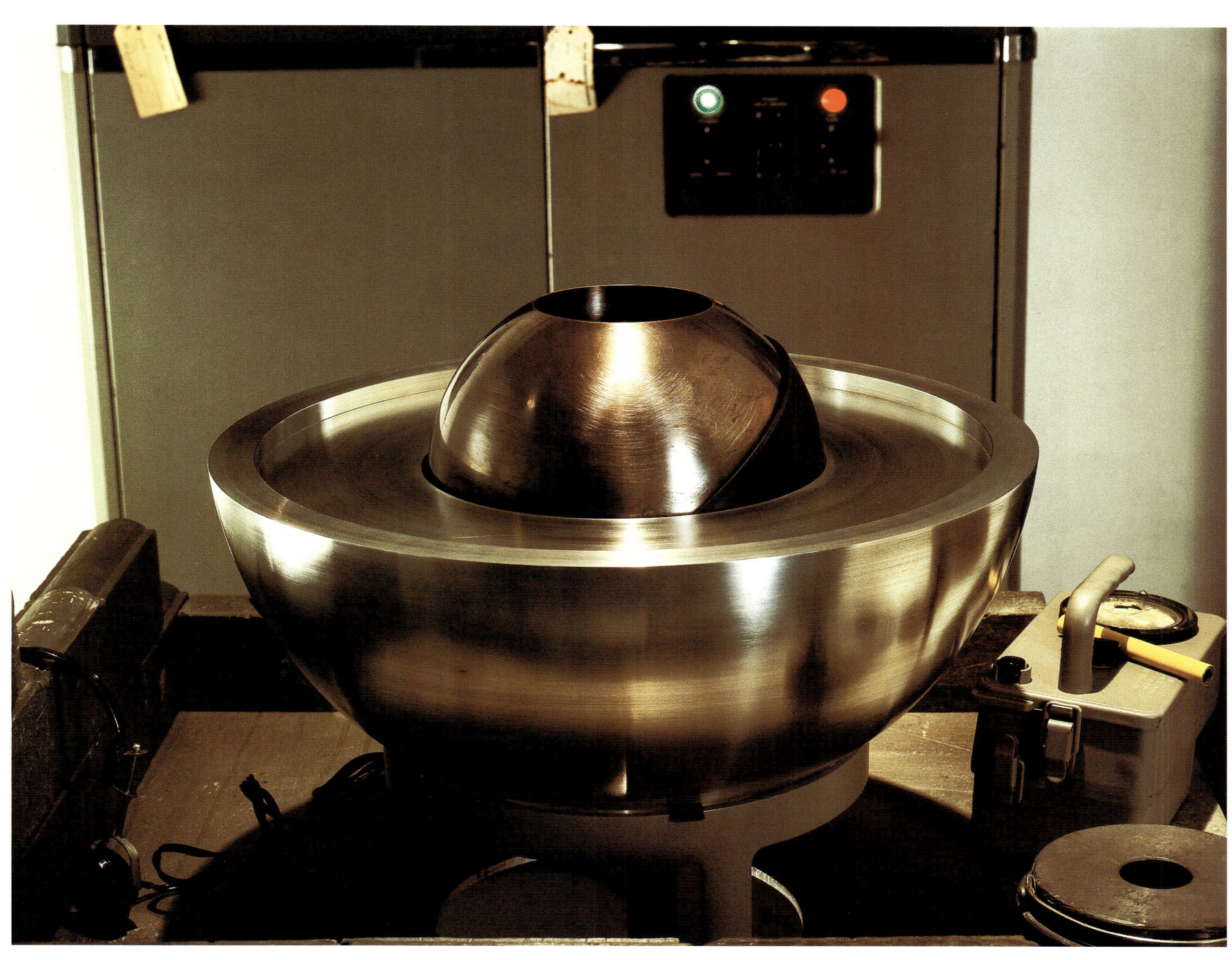

9. *Los Alamos G-M Counters and Electronics* (detail)
Electronic instruments
84 x 22 x 18", chassis dimensions

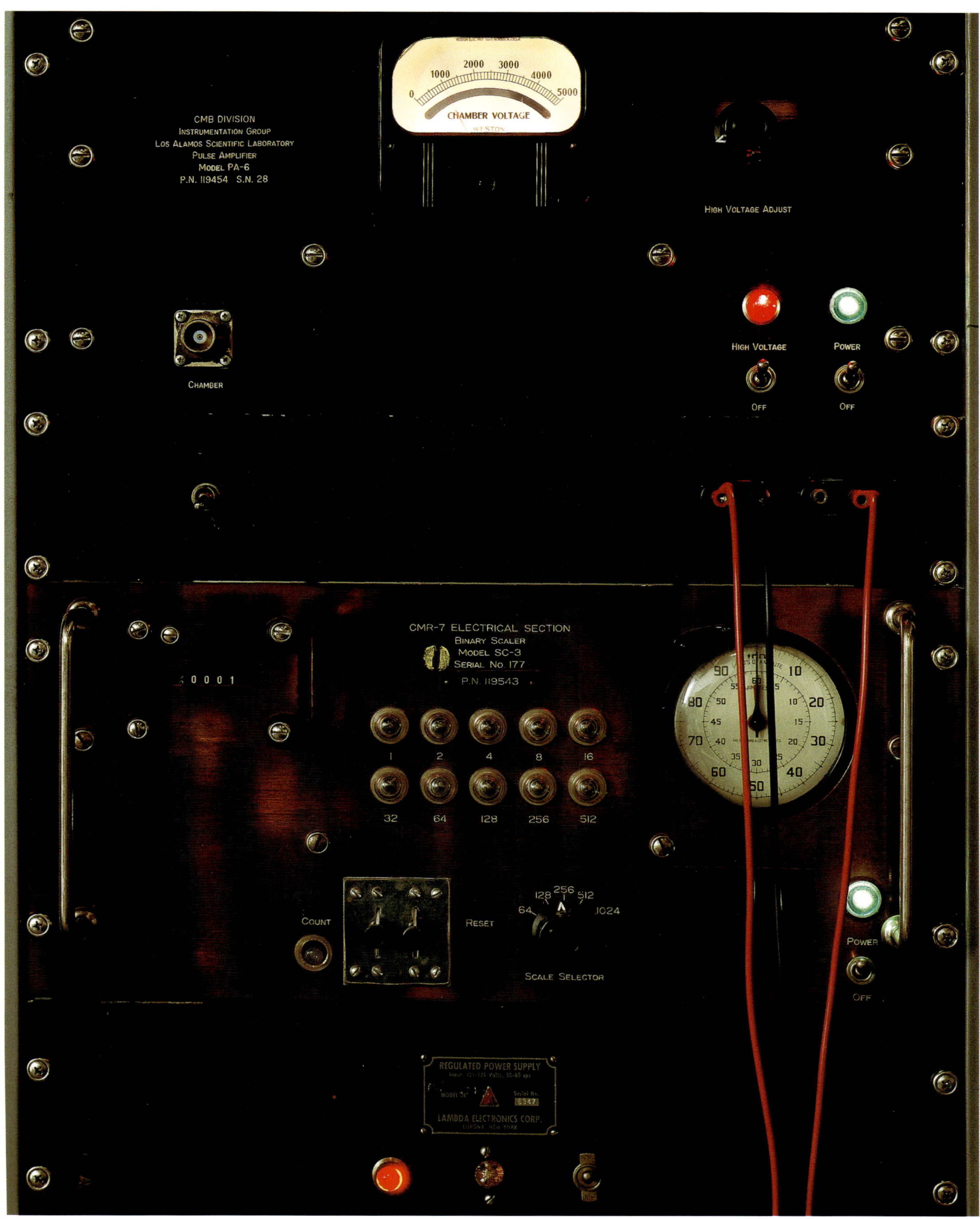
0
1000
2000
3000
4000
5000
CHAMBER VOLTAGE
CMB DIVISION
INSTRUMENTATION GROUP
LOS ALAMOS SCIENTIFIC LABORATORY
PULSE AMPLIFIER
MODEL PA-6
P.N. 119454 S.N. 28
HIGH VOLTAGE ADJUST
CHAMBER
HIGH VOLTAGE
POWER
OFF
OFF
CMR-7 ELECTRICAL SECTION
BINARY SCALER
MODEL SC-3
SERIAL NO. 177
P.N. 119543
1
2
4
8
16
32
64
128
256
512
COUNT
RESET
64
128
256
512
1024
SCALE SELECTOR
POWER
OFF
REGULATED POWER SUPPLY
LAMBDA ELECTRONICS CORP.

10. *Assembly for Determining Critical Mass*
Graphite blocks, tungsten carbide, stainless steel, chromium, silver-plated brass, detector probes, G-M counter, simulated hydraulic lift, wire, and sound
48 x 48 x 48", dimensions variable

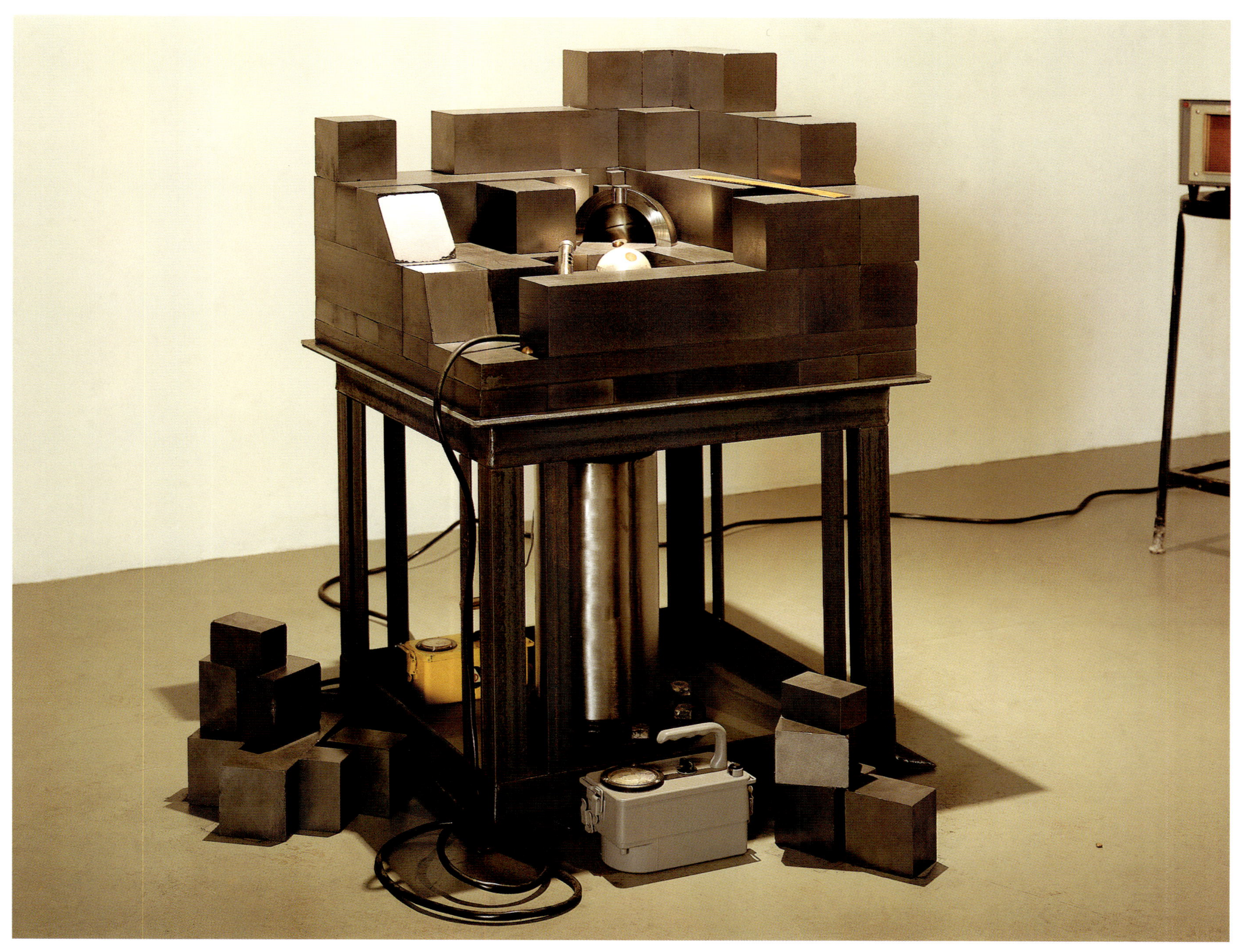

11. *Assembly for Determining Critical Mass* (detail)

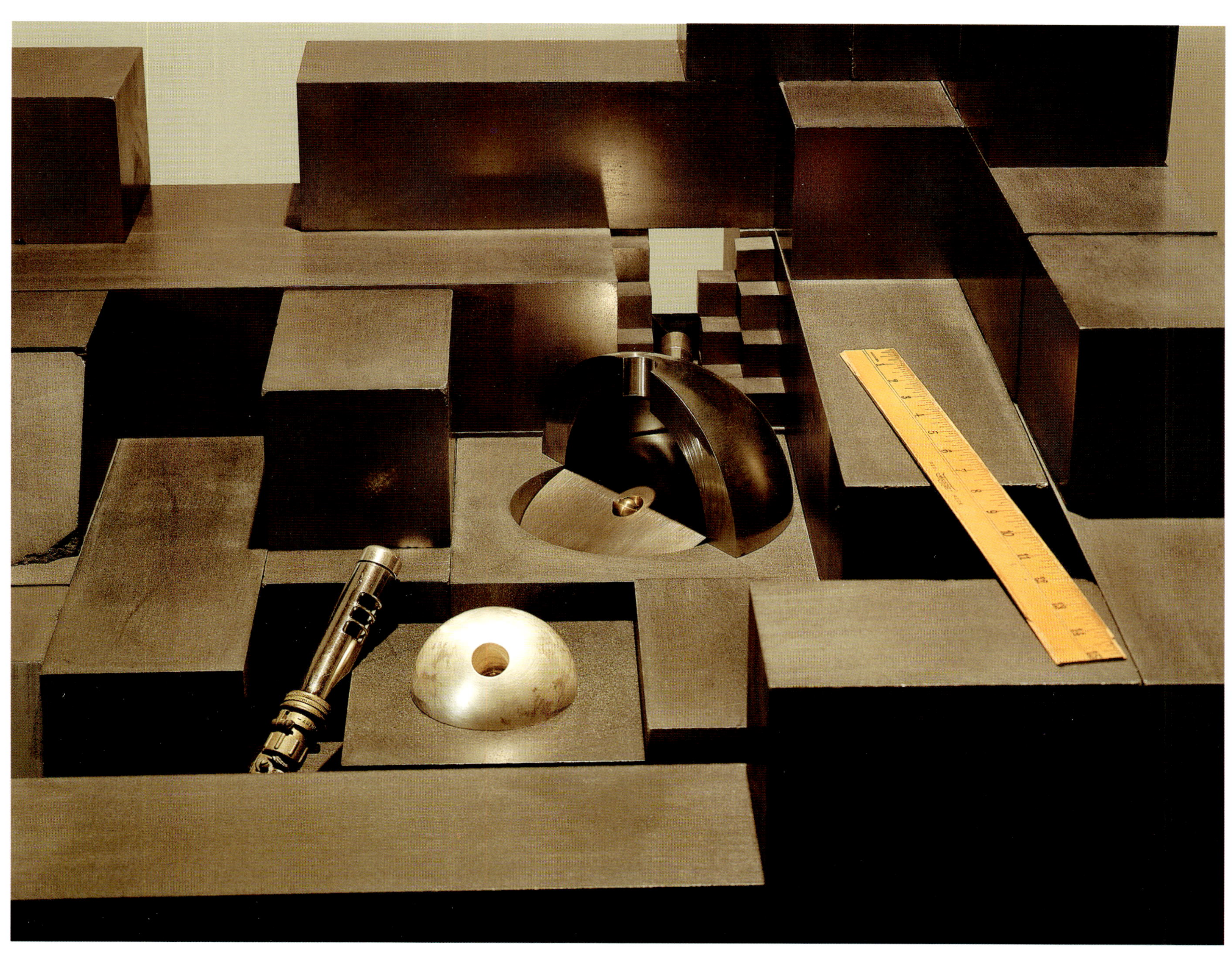

12. *Device for Measuring the Neutron Flux of a Uranium Core*
Paraffin blocks, chromium, stainless steel, brass, detector probes, oscilloscope, simulated hydraulic lift, wire, sound, and deuterium gas cylinder
48 x 70 x 48", dimensions variable

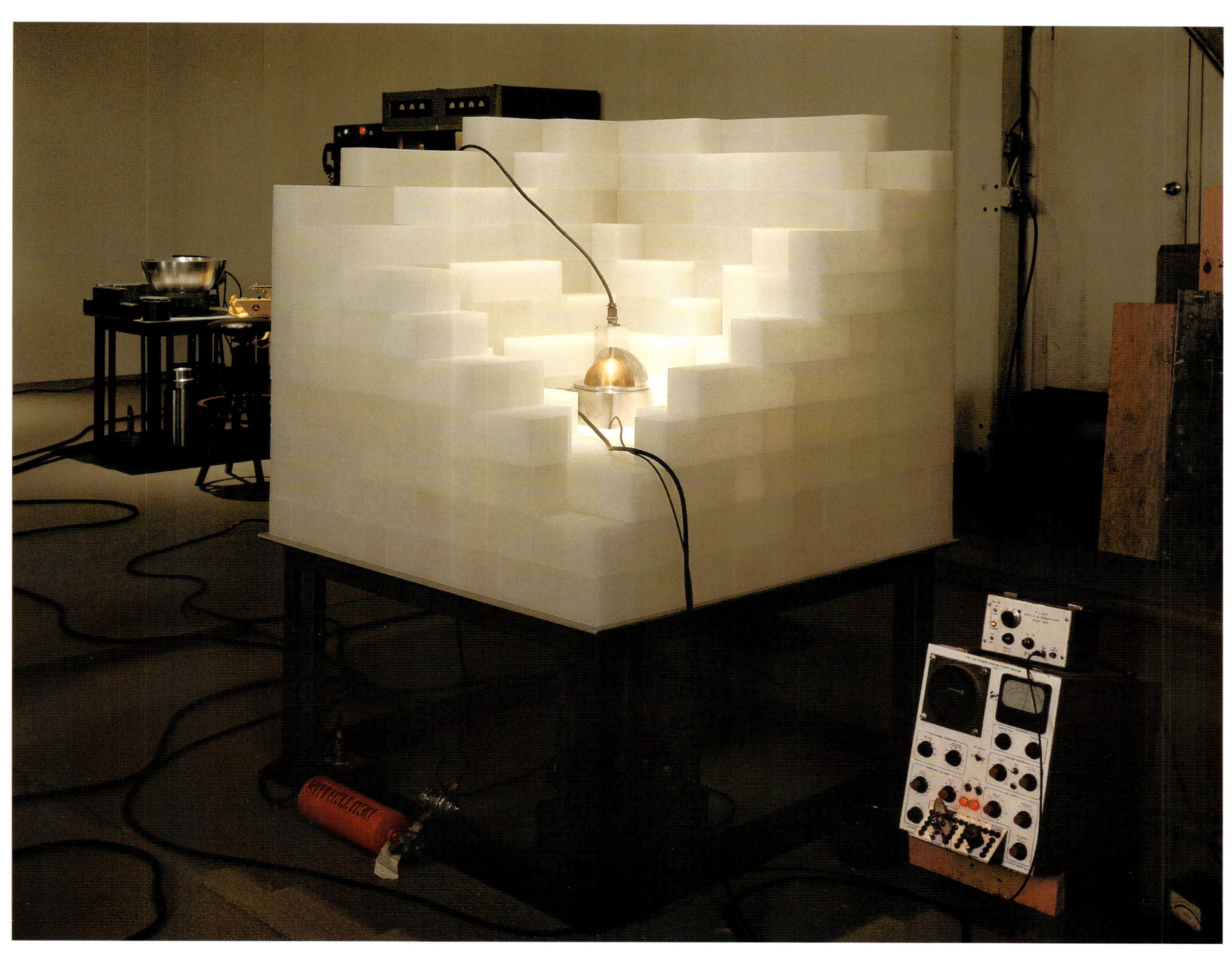

13. *Device for Measuring the Electromagnetic Flux of a Blast Wave* (detail)
Potentiometer, galvanometer, gamma counter, blueprint, lead, wood, aluminum, Los Alamos prototype, lead gloves, forged aluminum pusher sphere blanks, batteries, and aluminum machining table
40 x 72 x 36", dimensions variable

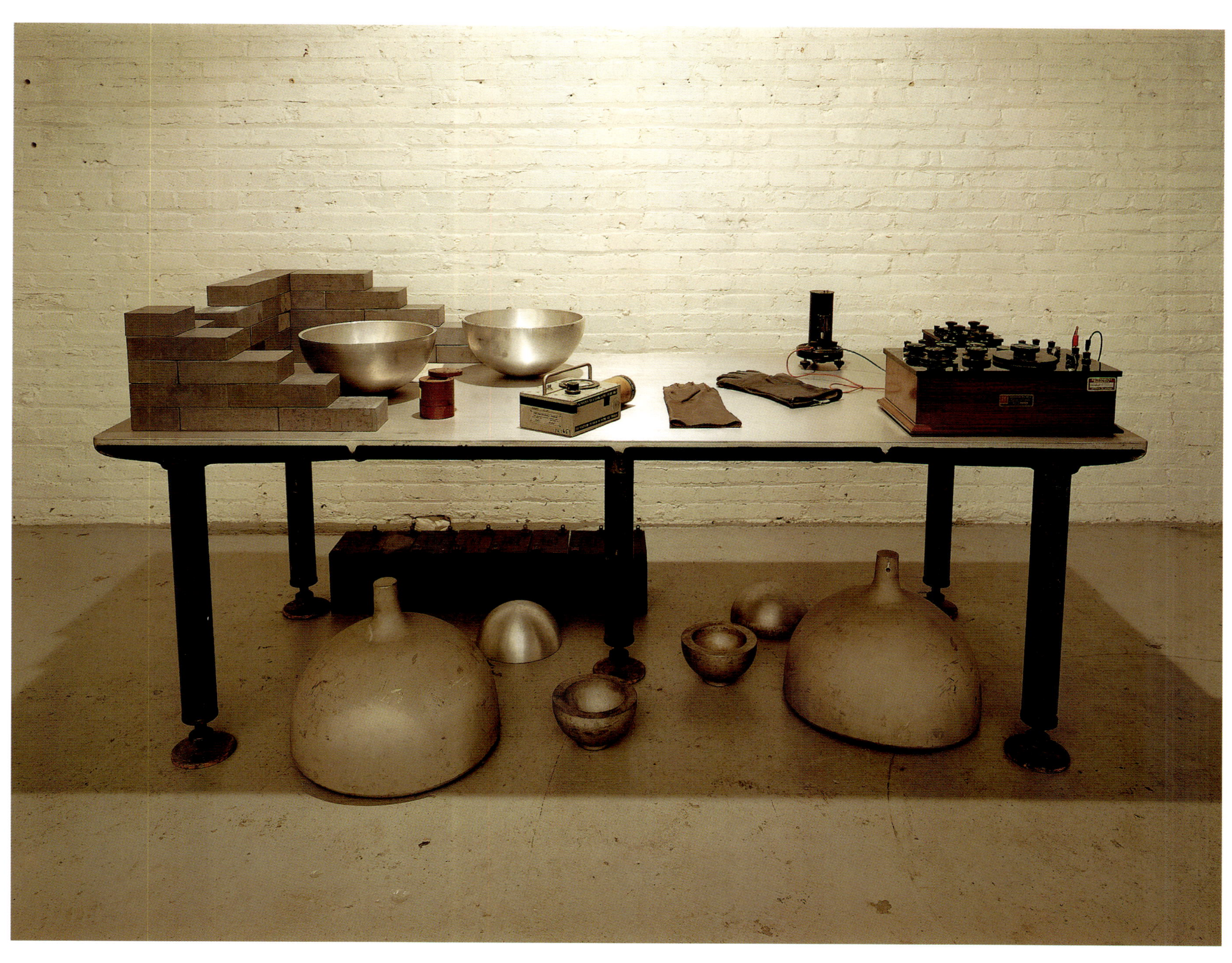

14. *Assembly for a Los Alamos Prototype II*
Los Alamos prototype, boron-impregnated polyethylene, lead, aluminum, graphite, G-M counters, detector probes, and wire
48 x 60 x 48", dimensions variable

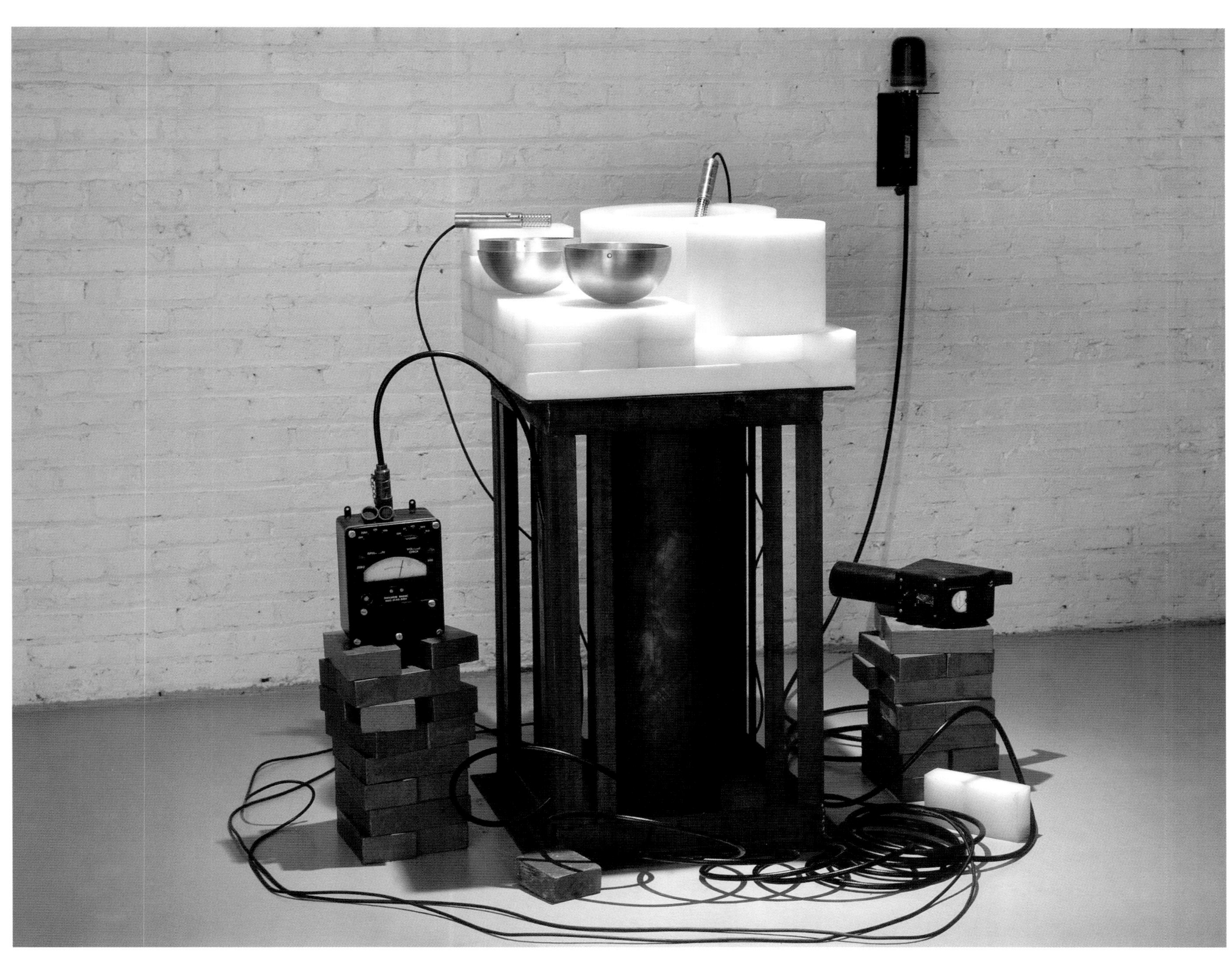

15. *Assembly for a Los Alamos Prototype II* (detail)

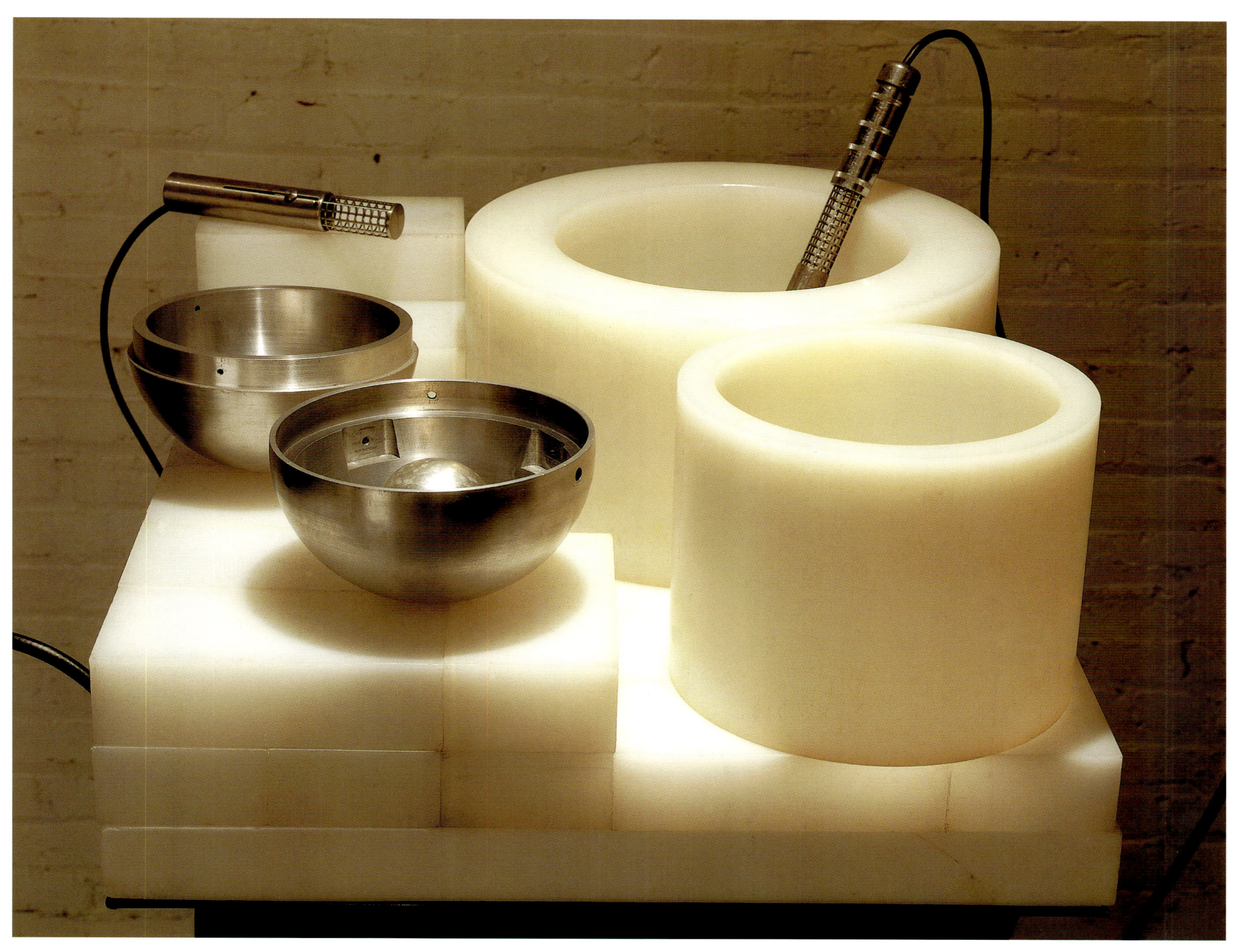

16. *Assembly for a Los Alamos Prototype I*
Wood table, Los Alamos prototype, graphite blocks, tungsten carbide, kraft paper, chromium, detector probes, G-M counters, wire, sound, and slide rule
84 x 72 x 60", dimensions variable

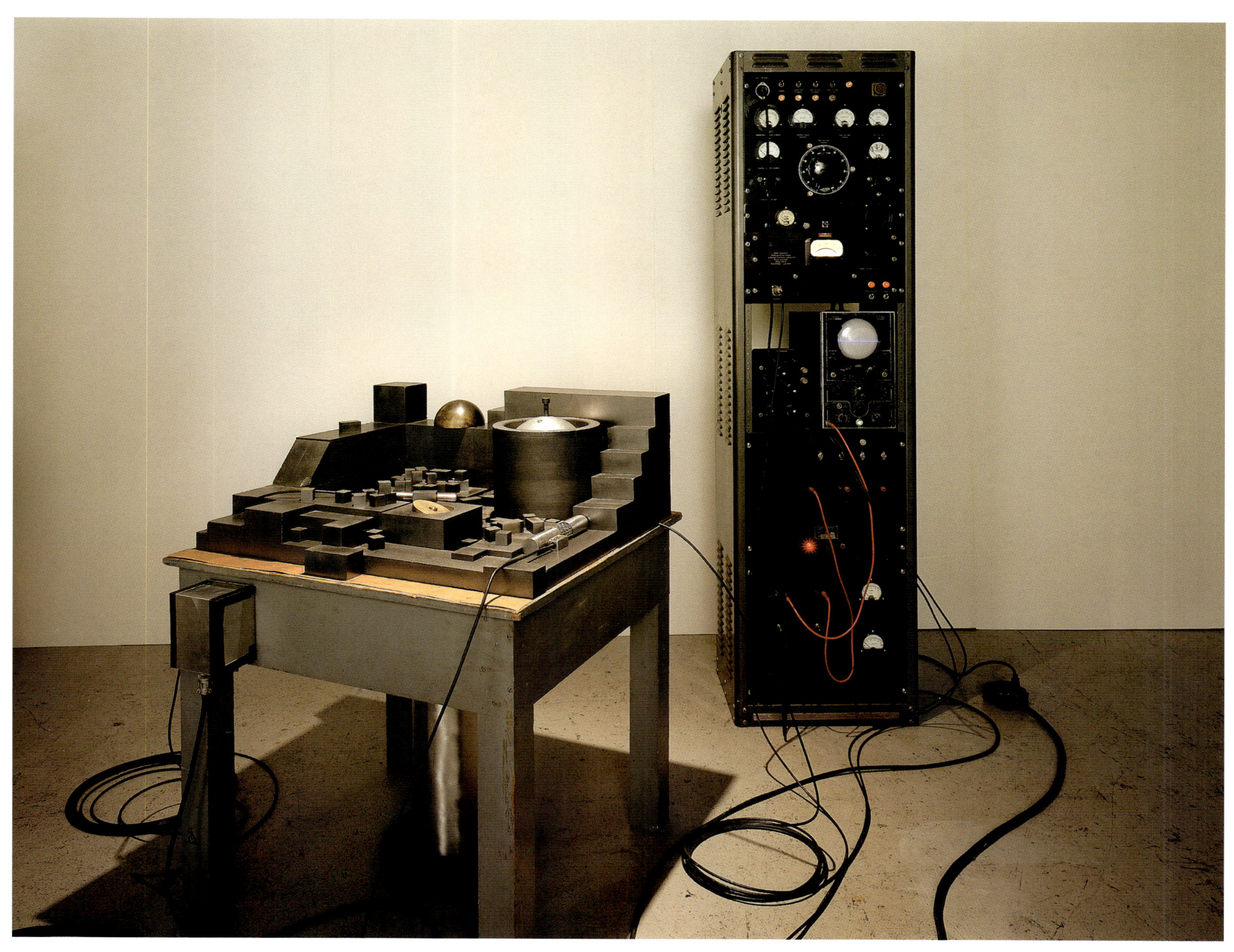

17. *Assembly for Determining the Critical Mass of a Hydride Cube*
Lead blocks, graphite, wood, particle discriminator, detector probes, tungsten carbide, chromium, G-M counter, simulated hydraulic lift, wire, sound, and ruler
60 x 72 x 48", dimensions variable

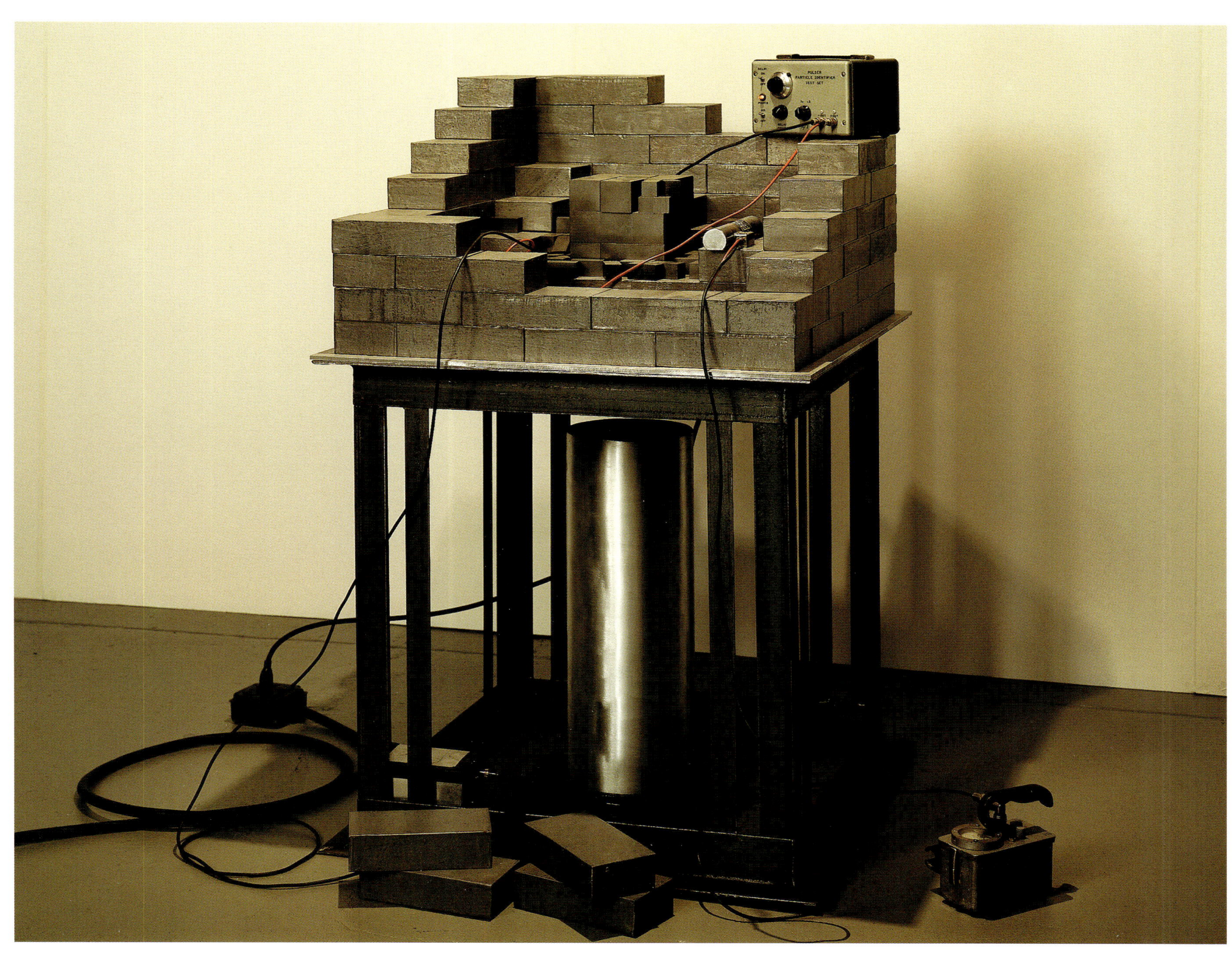
PULSER
PARTICLE IDENTIFIER
TEST SET

18. *Fermi's Assembly for Determining the Critical Mass of a Hemisphere*
Lead blocks, tungsten carbide, chromium, detector probes, G-M counter, wire, sound, and tape rule
54 x 48 x 60", dimensions variable

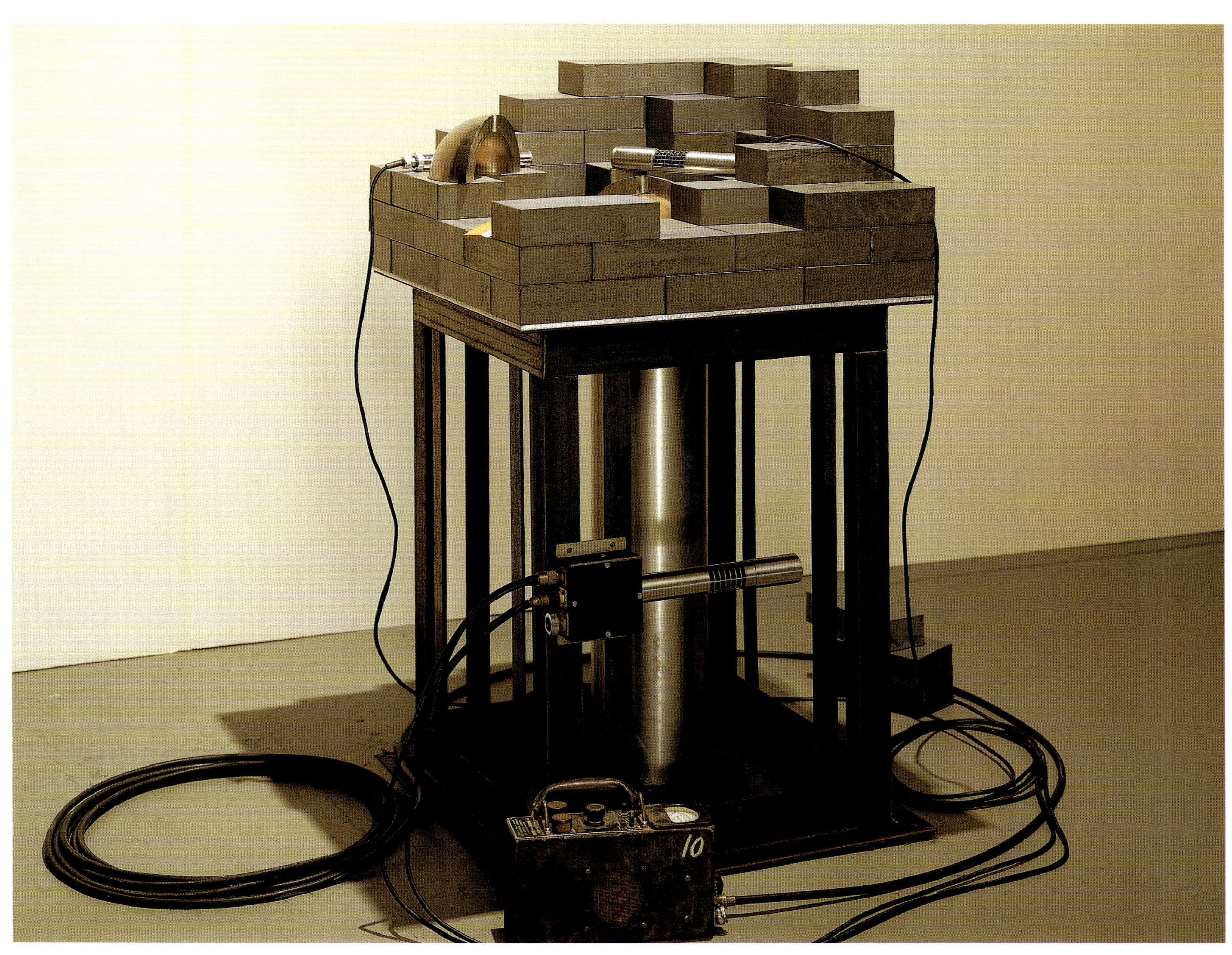
10

Tickling the Dragon's Tail

Howard Morland

In *Critical Assembly* (1998–2003), Jim Sanborn has re-created the moment in 1945 when human beings first fashioned a practical device powered by nuclear fission. It was called the "gadget." We know it today as the Trinity bomb. When it exploded on July 16 in the New Mexico desert, it permanently changed the human condition.

The place Sanborn takes us to is Los Alamos, in the 1940s a secret town known to the outside world only by its mailing address, Post Office Box 1663, Santa Fe, New Mexico. The scene is a small building in an isolated canyon, far enough from other buildings to contain the damage if the experimenters fry themselves with radiation, which two eventually do. On the tables are "criticality experiments," their purpose to determine how much plutonium 239 can be packed into a bomb for maximum yield without making the bomb unsafe to handle.[1]

The exercise is called "tickling the dragon's tail."

In 1978 I interviewed a man who conducted these experiments. He introduced himself by announcing, "I held the plutonium core of the Trinity bomb in my hands," and he offered his hands for inspection. He had built a nest of tungsten carbide blocks on a table and laid a plutonium ball in the center, like an egg waiting for incubation. Without so much as a lead apron for protection, he added blocks of nesting material as he listened to a loudspeaker connected to a neutron detector. He would put a small block on the corner of the table and slowly move it toward the assembly. An audible click meant a neutron had emerged from the plutonium ball and struck the detector. Several clicks in a short burst indicated that a neutron chain reaction had started in the plutonium but had died out. He would set the block in place and get another one. When several small blocks were safely in place, he would replace them with a full brick.

As the brick nest closed in over the egg, it started coming to life. When criticality was near, the mere presence of his hands over the assembly pushed it over the edge and made music on the loudspeaker. "My hands became part of the bomb," he said, as he offered his hands once again. "Ten fingers, and they all work."

The gadget's design concept was astonishingly simple. Plutonium can sustain a fast-fission chain reaction, that is, explode, merely by having enough of itself in the same place at the same time. The necessary amount is called a "critical mass." With pure plutonium metal in a solid sphere, critical mass is about the size of a baseball, three and a half inches in diameter. That fact had been determined by experiments like this one.

The completed gadget would employ, at its heart, a subcritical mass of plutonium, slightly smaller than a critical mass, surrounded by several concentric metal shells and five thousand pounds of high explosives, with thirty-two detonation points. When detonated, the high explosives would squeeze the plutonium like a soft rubber ball in a child's hand, increasing its density and converting the subcritical mass to a supercritical mass.[2] In this configuration, the explosive potential is equivalent to a three hundred-car freight train of TNT, much longer if the TNT is properly packaged for safe rail transportation. It would take two thousand B-29 bombers to carry this much explosive power in the form of TNT bombs.

The collage of experiments depicted here, in Sanborn's installation, adds up to a dress rehearsal for final assembly. The metallic components are in their final shape unless problems are detected. The plutonium baseball has a grape-sized cavity at its center. For experiments, this cavity holds a polonium-beryllium neutron source that supplies a constant neutron output; in the bomb it will hold the urchin, a similar component that releases its neutrons only when crushed by the implosive detonation of the bomb.

The plutonium is surrounded by a uranium 238 tamper shell two and a half inches thick, then a thin plastic and boron shell, and finally a four-inch-thick aluminum pusher shell. The shells assemble to form a sphere eighteen inches in diameter, except for a large cylindrical hole suggesting a cored apple, to allow insertion of the plutonium baseball at the last possible moment during assembly. The split cylinder that fills that hole and carries the plutonium to its central position in the gadget is composed of missing pieces from the concentric shells. When the cylinder is inserted, all the shells are complete.

The vast bulk of the finished gadget, which brings its diameter to five feet, is a double layer of high-explosive charges and an armored bomb casing to protect the falling bomb from antiaircraft flak. The high explosives and the steel casing were not part of the criticality experiments and are not shown in Sanborn's installation.

The exact amount of plutonium necessary for critical mass is influenced by the tendency of nearby materials to reflect free neutrons back into the plutonium. To avoid killing the assemblers, the subcritical plutonium must remain subcritical as extra stuff is packed around it. Thus the continuing need for these experiments, in which the extra stuff is simulated incrementally by blocks of paraffin or bricks of tungsten carbide. These tabletop barbecue pits allow the mock final assembly to be conducted cautiously, with the possibility of stopping the experiment as critical mass is approached.

By the summer of 1945, stopping the experiment was much on the mind of Leo Szilard (SIL-ard), the Hungarian physicist who had drafted Albert Einstein's 1939 letter to President Franklin D. Roosevelt. That letter initiated the Manhattan Project. But in Szilard's mind the need for a nuclear bomb had evaporated. Germany had surrendered in May of 1945, two months before the Trinity bomb was ready to be tested. Hitler was dead, and the Third Reich was out of business.

Szilard's purpose had been nuclear deterrence, not nuclear war. He saw America's nuclear bomb project as a guarantee against a German nuclear weapons monopoly, but Germany never got the bomb. To Szilard, and to other scientists in the Chicago and Oak Ridge branches of the Manhattan Project, the disappearance of the German nuclear threat changed everything.

Serving on a panel of seven Chicago scientists, chaired by chemist James Franck, he helped prepare a sixteen-page report, dated June 11, urging that the bomb not be used against Japan.[3] The members of the panel described themselves as "a small group of citizens cognizant of a grave danger for the safety of this country as well as for the future of all the other nations." They stated, "The rest of mankind is unaware" of this danger. Because nuclear weapons are so powerful, "protection can only come from the political organization of the world." They warned of a nuclear arms race if the bomb was used and said that "nuclear bombs cannot possibly remain a 'secret weapon' at the exclusive disposal of this country, for more than a few years."

On July 3, Szilard began circulating his own, similar petition, which declared that "atomic bombs are primarily a means for the ruthless annihilation of cities." He collected sixty-nine signatures at Chicago but was barred from seeking signatures at Los Alamos. A petition at Oak Ridge collected sixty-seven signatures. Very few people knew enough about the subject to have an opinion, but General Dwight Eisenhower and Admiral William Leahy were two who did, and they objected to the nuclear bombing of Japan.

All this controversy took place behind the same wall of secrecy that hid the continuing preparation of the bomb. Meanwhile, the people who actually controlled the project and made the decisions were focused on the task of finishing three bombs, one to test and two to drop on Japan. Tickling the dragon's tail confirmed theoretical assumptions about nuclear warhead design and allowed fine tuning, but its greatest significance may be simply that it continued. As long as these experiments were going on, the project was moving forward.

The experiments continued not only after the surrender of Germany but also after the surrender of Japan. The two fatal dragon-tail accidents at the Los Alamos laboratory took place during peacetime. The first was on August 21, 1945; the second was six months later, in the spring of 1946. The timing of these accidents lends credence to the theory that Russia had quickly replaced Germany and Japan as the rationale for a U.S. nuclear arsenal. There is no doubt that this happened soon

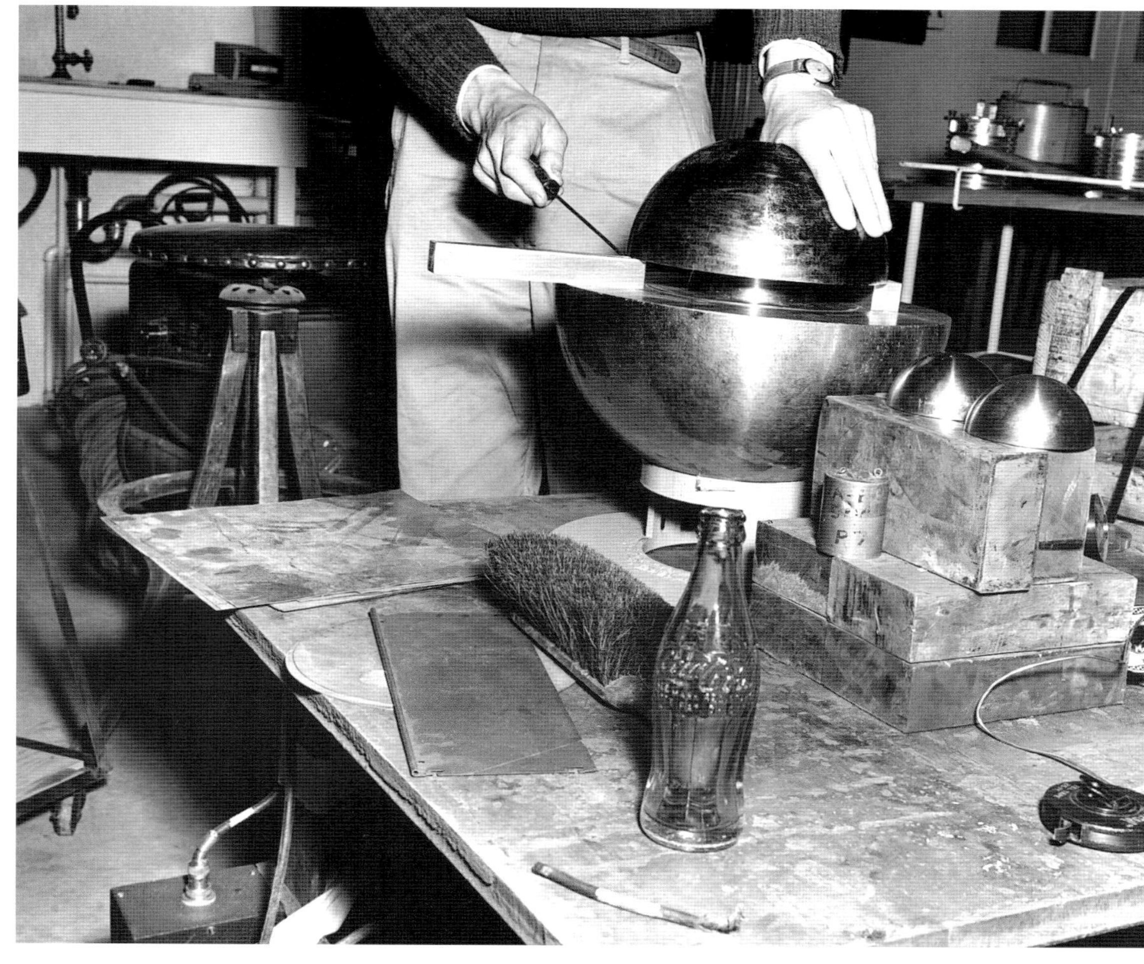

19. Los Alamos National Laboratory
1950s re-creation of the Slotin accident
Courtesy the Los Alamos National Laboratory

after the war, but some have argued that it happened during the war. The most persuasive advocates of this theory, by their actions, were the Los Alamos spies. No one has ever been accused of revealing nuclear secrets to Germany, Italy, or Japan. The spies at Los Alamos were working for an excluded ally, not an enemy.

Russia had at least three spy tracks going at Los Alamos: Klaus Fuchs, a British physicist in the top echelon; David Greenglass, a machinist who relayed less useful information through his brother-in-law Julius Rosenberg; and Theodore Alvin Hall, an eighteen-year-old Harvard graduate who was the youngest physicist in the Manhattan Project. After the war, Fuchs served prison time in Britain and then lived out his life behind the Iron Curtain. Julius and Ethel Rosenberg became perhaps the most famous spies in history when they were executed in 1953 on the basis of testimony by Greenglass, Ethel's brother. Unlike the other two, Hall was not an active Communist. He simply decided on his own that the United States should not be trusted with a nuclear weapons monopoly. He sensed that the United States and Russia would soon be rival superpowers and believed that Russia needed a nuclear deterrent. His volunteer spying was concealed for fifty years, and he was never prosecuted.[4]

The role of Hiroshima and Nagasaki in ending World War II will be debated forever. Did the nuclear destruction of those two cities obviate the need for a bloody invasion of Japan, or was the war effectively over by that time? Was the bombing of Japan as much a message to Russia as it was to Japan, as some have argued? There will never be consensus on that question, but certain facts are beyond dispute.

No advocate for bombing Japan argued that the country still had military assets that could not be destroyed by conventional means. Everyone agreed that the purpose of dropping the bomb would be to demonstrate its effect on an undamaged city—to kill civilians in their homes—and that the impact would be psychological, not military. It is widely believed that this acknowledged act of terror shortened the war and saved more lives than it destroyed. Those who argue otherwise will always face a storm of criticism.[5]

However, the Manhattan Project produced much more than three bombs. It left in place a huge industry able to mass-produce nuclear bombs. The immense processing plants at Oak Ridge, Tennessee, and Hanford, Washington, were not fully up and running until the end of the war. By the late summer of 1945, they had produced enough fissile uranium and plutonium for three bombs, but they didn't stop when the war ended. The bomb was clearly destined to be around long after World War II was over.

When Harry Daghlian fried himself on August 21, a week after the Japanese surrender, he knew he was working on a bomb intended for use against Russia. His death was a 1945 Cold War casualty. He was cutting corners, holding a full brick of tungsten carbide over a criticality experiment that was only half a brick shy of critical. When the loudspeaker went nuts, he jerked back his hand and dropped the brick on the pile. The burst of radiation that mortally wounded him turned the air in the room blue. He lived twenty-eight days; he was conscious the whole time. His colleague Louis Slotin sat with him as he died.

The plutonium core Daghlian was working with was so little affected that its nickel cladding was not ruptured. It survived to kill Slotin himself in a similar accident on May 21, 1946 (fig. 19). This time the reflector material was a beryllium shell that Slotin was holding with a screwdriver. The screwdriver slipped, the shell dropped over the plutonium, and the air turned blue. Slotin knew from Daghlian's experience that there was nothing left of his life but to watch himself die, which took nine days. Once again the plutonium core was not damaged.

These criticality experiments continued for decades without interruption, but never again on tables with experimenters standing over them. After Slotin, they were done by remote control, with the workers in well-shielded safe rooms a quarter mile away.

Anyone with an eye for shape can see aesthetic value in finely machined metallic hemispheres bisected by a cylinder. The contrast between the clean lines of the bomb parts and the tripping hazard of random cables on the floor suggests an artist's studio where everything is a mess except the painting. But why would an artist choose this subject? Why put a replica of a nuclear bomb's internal components on public display for the first time ever? Is *Critical Assembly* an artistic glorification of a weapon of mass murder? Is it an invitation for nuclear terrorists to take notes and threaten nuclear destruction? Is it art? And if so, is it art gone too far?

Any human event can capture an artist's imagination: a woman sitting by a window or a day in a Flemish seaport. When the event has historic significance, like Julius Caesar crossing the Rubicon or Columbus landing in America, there is strong incentive to embellish. But we live in an age of documentation. We know that General Douglas McArthur's wading ashore in the Philippines during World War II was a staged event, a photo opportunity. Our culture has an appetite for stark reality, the truth behind the image, except, perhaps, when the subject is nuclear weapons.

Declasssified photographs of the Los Alamos criticality experiments show the room and its environment but hide the experimental apparatus behind a sheet (fig. 2). A famous photograph of the gadget shows it half disassembled, back to the eighteen-inch sphere, but its internal components remain hidden: the pusher, the boron, the tamper, the core, and the urchin. In *Critical Assembly*, the shapes of these heretofore hidden components, which means the thickness of each shell, come from the fifty-year-old memories of technicians who handled the split cylinder that contained a piece of each shell. With their help, Sanborn finishes peeling the onion.

Is that really necessary? In theory, it should be the artist's call, but no one wants to jeopardize public safety. A simple appeal to artistic license and freedom of speech will not satisfy everyone. I have personal experience defending this kind of expression in a court of law. My 1979 article on the hydrogen bomb was tied up in court for six months. In the case of *USA vs. The Progressive, et al.*, a

NOTES

1. Official accounts of the Los Alamos criticality experiments and the Daghlian and Slotin accidents are found in two Los Alamos studies: William R. Stratton, "A Review of Criticality Accidents" [LA-3611 UC-46 Criticality Studies TID-4500], 1967, and Richard E. Malenfant, "Lessons Learned From Early Criticality Accidents" [LA-UR-96-1659], 1996. The stories are also told in most Manhattan Project histories, starting with Robert Jungk, *Brighter than a Thousand Suns: A Personal History of the Atomic Scientists*, translated by James Cleugh (New York: Harcourt Brace Jovanovich, 1958; published in Germany in 1956).

2. Dimensions and shapes of the nuclear bomb components depicted in Sanborn's installation come from John Coster-Mullen, *Atomic Bombs: The Top Secret Inside Story of Little Boy and Fat Man*, which the author self-published in manuscript form in 2002. Extensively researched, with thirty pages of endnotes for eighty pages of text, his book draws on all the relevant information in the open literature. Coster-Mullen adds to that literature the fruit of scores of interviews he conducted with Los Alamos technicians and with men of the 509th Composite Group who assembled the bombs and dropped them on Japan. This unique resource makes his account a nuts-and-bolts story, told from the viewpoint of the men who handled the hardware.

3. The Franck Report and Szilard's petitions are posted online under "Atomic Bomb: Decision [Hiroshima-Nagasaki]" at *http://www.dannen.com/decision/index.html.*

4. The brief spying career of Theodore Alvin Hall was revealed by KGB files that became public after the fall of the Soviet Union. The story is told in Joseph Albright and Marcia Kunstel, *Bombshell: The Secret Story of America's Unknown Atomic Spy Conspiracy* (New York: Times Books, 1997).

5. The controversy over the use of nuclear bombs against Hiroshima and Nagasaki, which began in secret in the summer of 1945, continues to this day. Two recent books outline the opposing arguments: Richard B. Frank, in *Downfall: The End of the Imperial Japanese Empire* (New York: Random House, 1999),

civil lawsuit, the federal government imposed prior restraint on my written speculations and schematic drawings about H-bomb design. Our ultimately successful defense was based on two themes: that my information was already public knowledge and that my description was neither accurate enough nor complete enough to be helpful to bomb builders.[6]

Ideally, First Amendment freedom should cover Sanborn's right to show this installation in museums around the world. A legal defense, should one be required, might take the same tack as *The Progressive* case. The information on bomb design that he presents in graphic form in *Critical Assembly* is already public knowledge, and it is neither as accurate nor as complete as it seems to be.

However, that bit of legalism glosses over an important fact: a crude nuclear weapon is not difficult to build. It's just layers of material. Any number of designs will work, so long as they quickly aggregate a supercritical mass of fissile material, plutonium 239 or uranium 235, and hold it together against its tendency to blow apart when heated.

The Little Boy bomb, which used a gun barrel to fire one chunk of uranium into another, was considered so simple and reliable that it was dropped on Hiroshima without ever having been tested. It worked. Fat Man, the Nagasaki bomb, was a copy of the plutonium-implosion Trinity bomb that was test-fired in New Mexico on July 16, where it, too, worked on the first try. It is nonsense to suppose that a nation capable of producing fissile uranium or plutonium will have any trouble making a bomb.

Control of nuclear material, not information, is the key to nuclear nonproliferation. In my view, there is no harm in demonstrating how easy it is to make nuclear weapons. On the contrary, it shows the importance of controlling the essential ingredients. Unlike information, fissile material cannot be photocopied, spread by word of mouth, or posted on a Web site. It is real stuff, a physical substance, very expensive to make and dangerous to handle, and you can't make a nuclear bomb without it.

J. Robert Oppenheimer, the scientific director of the Manhattan Project, is the man who prevented the Szilard petition from circulating at Los Alamos. Within his inner circle, he argued that inviting observers to a nuclear bomb test in the desert, as the Franck Report urged, would not produce enough shock value to end the war. In his opinion, a city full of people needed to be destroyed, without warning, to properly demonstrate the power of the bomb.[7] However, when he saw the Trinity fireball rise into the New Mexico sky on July 16, he recalled a passage from the Hindu scripture, the Bhagavad Gita, which he translated: "Now I am become death, the destroyer of worlds." He supposed they all thought that, one way or another.

There's an interesting thing about that passage. The only reference to world destruction in the Bhagavad Gita comes in verse thirty-two of chapter eleven, which is usually translated: "The Lord said, 'I am Time grown old to destroy the world, Embarked on the course of world annihilation.'" In the Bhagavad Gita, time (*kalah*), not death (*mrtyuh*), is the destroyer of worlds. When Oppenheimer watched the Trinity fireball create a false dawn in New Mexico, what he saw was time running out. A doomsday clock had started to tick.[8]

Every viewer will find a political message in *Critical Assembly*. I see a reminder that nuclear weapons are the work of human hands. Since its invention, the nuclear bomb has seemed to have a life of its own. It has survived numerous changes of rationale: the potential German bomb, the Japanese reluctance to surrender, the Communist threat, the Capitalist threat (from the Communist point of view), and finally the threat of the bomb itself. The last two decades of the Cold War saw a futile search for ways to make nuclear weapons cancel each other out, and for ways to defeat such imaginary self-cancellation.

In all that confusion, hype, and terror, it was easy to forget that nuclear weapons are assembled. They don't grow on trees or in the blood of infected people. They are hardware, handiwork. They can be disassembled.

reiterates the standard argument that the bombs saved lives by ending the war before the scheduled invasion of Japan; Gar Alperovitz, in *The Decision to Use the Atomic Bomb: And the Architecture of an American Myth* (New York: Alfred A. Knopf, 1995), argues that neither the bombs nor an invasion was necessary to secure the Japanese surrender. When the Smithsonian Institution's National Air and Space Museum scheduled an exhibit in 1995 that would have explored all aspects of the Hiroshima and Nagasaki bombings, a campaign by the Air Force Association, the American Legion, and the *Washington Post* forced the cancellation of the exhibit before it opened. Two accounts of that brouhaha are *Hiroshima's Shadow: Writings on the Denial of History and the Smithsonian Controversy,* edited by Kai Bird and Lawrence Lifschutz (Stony Creek, Conn.: The Pamphleteer's Press, 1998), and the Air Force Association's Web page, "The Enola Gay and the Smithsonian, Chronology of the Controversy Including Key Documents, 1993–1995," posted at *http://www.afa.org/media/enolagay.chrono.asp.*

6. The 1979 case of *USA vs. The Progressive, et al.*, is examined in my Web article, "The Holocaust Bomb, a Question of Time," updated at *http://www.fas.org/sgp/eprint/morland.html*, along with references and links to sources and documents.

7. On June 16, 1945, Oppenheimer explained to scientists at Los Alamos why he believed a Japanese city should be bombed without warning. See Gregg Herken, *Brotherhood of the Bomb: The Tangled Lives and Loyalties of Robert Oppenheimer, Ernest Lawrence, and Edward Teller* (New York: Henry Holt, 2002).

8. The Bhagavad Gita quote is from 11:32, translation by J.A.B. Van Buitenen, introduction by Alexandre Piatigorsky (Rockport, Mass.: Element Books, 1997). Another translation, with English and Sanskrit juxtaposed, is posted on the Web at *http://www.iskcon.org/sastra/f_bg.html*. Of the six translations I have seen, only one translates this passage as Oppenheimer did. In all the others, the word *kalah*, or *kalo*, in the line "kalo 'smi loka-ksaya-krt pravrttah," is translated as "time," not "death." Generally, where the word death appears in the English translation, such as 9:3, 9:19, 10:34, and 13:9, the Sanskrit word is *mrtyuh*, not *kalah*.

The Nature of Secrets—The Secrets of Nature

Barbara London

The entrance and inner courtyard of the Central Intelligence Agency headquarters in Langley, Virginia, feature components of Jim Sanborn's work *Kryptos* (1988–90). One section of the installation, at the entrance, is anchored by a large petrified tree trunk. Petrifaction is a mysterious process, and despite many attempts, scientists have been unable to produce petrified wood (or bone) in a lab. In essence, Sanborn parked a big question mark on the CIA's lawn as an antidote to hubris. As CIA employees stream into the office at Langley, *Kryptos* exhorts them to remember human limitations and to devise their plans accordingly.

Another part of the work, in the courtyard, underscores Sanborn's provocative intent. A large S-shaped copper screen is perforated with letters of the English alphabet lined up as a strange text (fig. 20). The inscription is a cipher. Sanborn reportedly refused to reveal the message and chided the CIA for failing to break the code. He stood his ground until the dedication of the work and then handed over a partial decipherment to William Webster, then director of the CIA. The message has still not been fully deciphered, and thus the work remains a challenge and an enigma.

Sanborn's venture into the shadowy realm of secrecy continues in a work about the atomic bomb. *Critical Assembly* (1998–2003) depicts many features formerly stamped "Top Secret." The artist

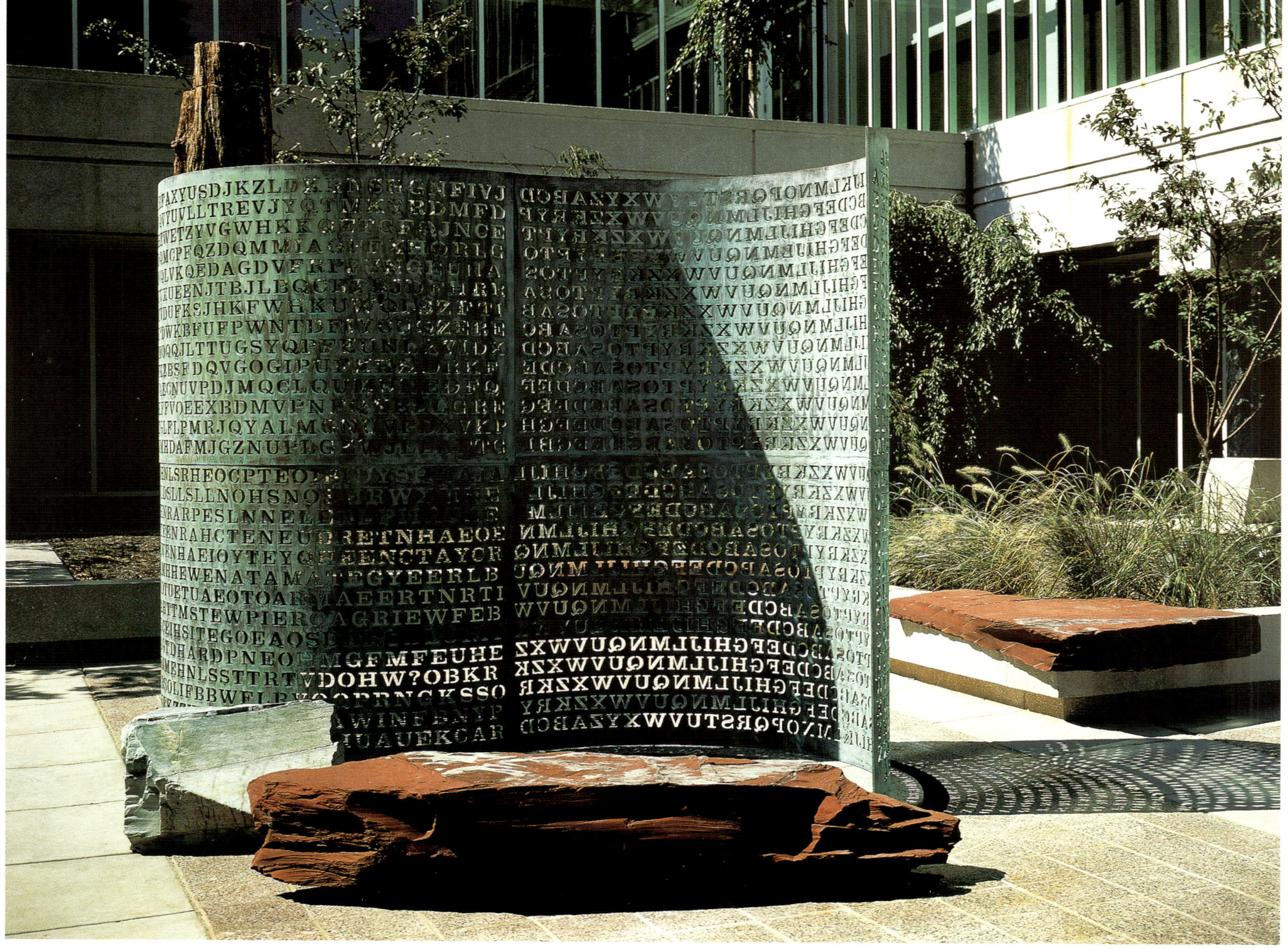

20. *Kryptos*, 1988–90
Copper, quartz, slate, petrified tree, myscanthus grasses, encoded text, and water
11 x 20 x 10'
View of inner courtyard
Collection of Central Intelligence Agency, Langley, Va.

argues that his version of the bomb does not reveal classified information, and he further insists that there are no atomic secrets. He supports this assertion with two massive books published in the 1980s, one by Richard Rhodes and the other by Howard Morland.[1] They describe in detail the technology of the early versions of atomic and hydrogen bombs, respectively. In 1979 the U.S. government tried to block publication of an earlier essay by Morland that led to his book-length study, but the courts ruled that the relevant information had appeared previously in journals and thus was in the public domain.

The government's penchant for secrecy has often been the subject of Sanborn's work. He regards secrecy as a tool that certain people in positions of power sometimes use to enhance their authority. Those in charge of producing and safeguarding atomic weapons gain influence by building a wall of secrecy around their operations. Sanborn claims that the focus on atomic secrecy is counterproductive, because it deflects attention from the only significant barrier to fabricating the bomb. Access to fissionable material and processing equipment is all that stands in the way of building atomic weapons.

Current events seem to bear out Sanborn's contention. The how-to of making the bomb is widespread, and antiproliferation efforts are now directed toward gathering up and eliminating radioactive feedstock. However, more than a recipe and the right ingredients enter into the fabrication of the bomb. Before the task begins, there must be an incentive to undertake the effort. Harnessing the power of an atomic bomb may entail obscure personal dynamics.

Sanborn tells the little-known tale of an American teenager who assembled a large quantity of intensely radioactive material. The youngster bought up old clocks with luminous radium dials and amassed a radioactive cache one scrap at a time. The story is typically American, suitable for a Norman Rockwell painting updated as a video. The youngster, a high school student in a small midwestern town, is seated on a cot in a simply furnished bedroom. He buttons his striped pajamas, switches off the lights, and opens the drawer of a night table. An eerie green light from a glowing vial of radium illuminates the young scientist's face. He gazes upon his treasure with the innocent anticipation of a toddler looking at presents under a Christmas tree. He reluctantly shuts the drawer and rolls into bed. A sigh expresses the contentment of this regular American kid as he leaves behind his real-life fantasy and passes into the dream realm where fantasies abound.

The structure where Sanborn built his installation is a single-story nondescript warehouse in an industrial section of Washington, D.C., far from prying eyes. To a visitor, the studio is disorienting. Metal tables with bizarre appendages, walls of white paraffin bricks, and paraphernalia suspended by chains hint at arcane experiments. Tall racks of blinking electronic gear provide a familiar laboratory backdrop to the clutter. When Sanborn picks up a Geiger counter wand, and its clicks detecting background radiation begin, the setting takes on an aura of quintessential mystery. The flat, unexceptional clicks are chilling, as if atoms were conveying the coded message that nature's most dreadful secrets are banal. The metal guts of Sanborn's version of the Trinity bomb seem benign. The shiny nested spheres have no apparent connection to the destructive power of an atomic bomb. Only the reprise of Geiger counter clicks sounds a warning that something peculiar is afoot.

A Sanborn guided tour of the bomb is exhaustive. He does not withhold information, yet he seems reticent. A visitor's enthusiastic interest elicits more information, but the discussion appears to increase Sanborn's discomfort. Surely, the release of nonsecrets about the bomb cannot be the source of his malaise. He has battled government secrecy. Moreover, the Trinity bomb is many decades old, and no bomb-maker today would use the ancient technology.

The discoveries Sanborn made in researching the bomb now weigh on him. Not only does he know the theory behind making an atomic bomb, he knows how to go about doing it. Sanborn fears and feeds on the urge that led him to find out more than he is comfortable with knowing. He recognizes in himself the insatiable curiosity that impels scientists and artists to see what's over the next hill.

Artists and scientists often court danger in pursuing their ambitions. Leonardo was vilified for raiding cemeteries to get cadavers for his anatomical sketches. Although the science of anatomy, and medicine in general, has developed in astounding ways since the days of Leonardo, experimentation on the human body remains a taboo. Today genetic engineering, cloning, and stem cells are proscribed areas of medical research. Modern biological research arouses passions reminiscent of the zealous efforts in Leonardo's time to block grave robbing and the dissection of corpses.

Humans seek knowledge, yet they are chary of the power knowledge entails. This ambivalence is as old as the story of Adam and Eve snacking on an apple. At the very beginning of history, man and woman were warned of dire consequences if they acquired knowledge of good and evil. The wily serpent induced them to eat of the tree of knowledge, and thereby humankind lost the bliss that unawareness bestows. The narrative teaches that man and woman sought knowledge rather than heed a higher authority, and consequently they have to live by their wits, for better or for worse.

A museum setting provides an appropriate context for *Critical Assembly*. The installation is clean and focused, without emotional cues or other artistic intrusions that distract from a central theme—the minimalism of the bomb. The device belies the scientific genius that went into its development and the dread it engenders. Its innocuous appearance is chilling, yet the very nakedness of the bomb sends the mind spinning to basic questions about life and nature. *Critical Assembly* serves to strip away historical baggage and encourage a rethinking of entrenched attitudes about the atomic age.

The term *atomic age* is no longer in fashion. From the end of World War II until the 1980s, great debates raged over the use of atomic energy. The image of a mushroom cloud was seared into human consciousness. The landscape of Hiroshima flattened by the bomb was widely recognized, and photos of domed reactor chambers for generating electricity were common. Missing from the picture was a reasoned plan for a future where atomic energy and society could coexist harmoniously.

The history of atomic energy chronicles a colossal failure of the human enterprise. Einstein's early-twentieth-century discovery of the relation between mass and energy promised an era of free energy that would fuel a paradisiacal earth. The media in the early 1950s assured a world dispirited by the devastation of war that better days were coming. Plastic and the atom would build a future where human wants were fully satisfied.

Regrettably, military and commercial interests gained control of atomic development, and the lofty vision collapsed. The creative potential disappeared amid calculations of profit and loss and plans for defense and destruction. Rational dialogue degenerated into an ongoing confrontation that pitted antinuclear activists against vested interests. Thorny issues such as how to handle nuclear waste received a good deal of media attention but limited scientific research. The troubling consequences of Einstein's discovery have yet to be resolved.

Sanborn offers a novel way of perceiving the bomb. He puts the viewer in direct contact with the naked device and the womb that gave it existence. A viewer contemplating *Critical Assembly* does not see an instrument of terrible destruction, but instead encounters a mystery of creation manifested in the nested metal spheres attended by cables, irregular lights, and staccato sounds. The installation encourages a reexamination of atomic energy from its inception.

Critical Assembly serves as an advisory in much the same way that Sanborn's sculpture at CIA headquarters does. *Kryptos* challenges the employees at Langley, exhorting them to mull over the fundamental premise of their work—the nature of secrets. *Critical Assembly* reaches out to a wider public, to anyone who contemplates the secrets of nature. The work is bound to invigorate the thinking of people who wonder where the current age of discovery is heading.

NOTE

1. Richard Rhodes, *The Making of the Atomic Bomb* (New York: Simon & Schuster, 1986); and Howard Morland, *The Secret that Exploded* (New York: Random House, 1981).

Atomic Time

21. *Joachimsthal, Bavaria,* 2001
Uranium autoradiograph

All works are by Jim Sanborn, Ilfachrome prints, 30 x 36" each.
Courtesy the artist and Numark Gallery, Washington, D.C.

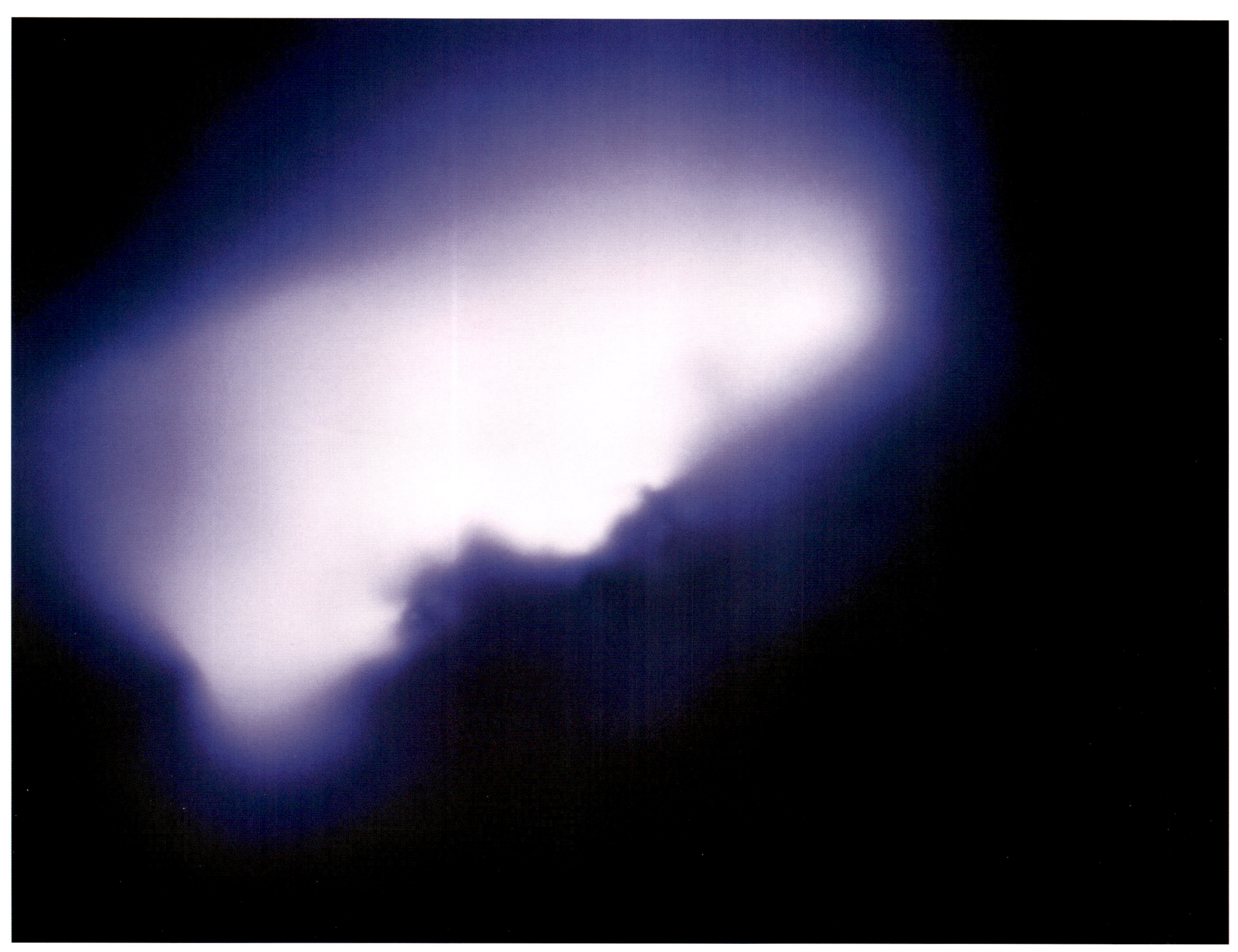

22. *Gas Hills, Wyoming,* 2001
Uranium autoradiograph

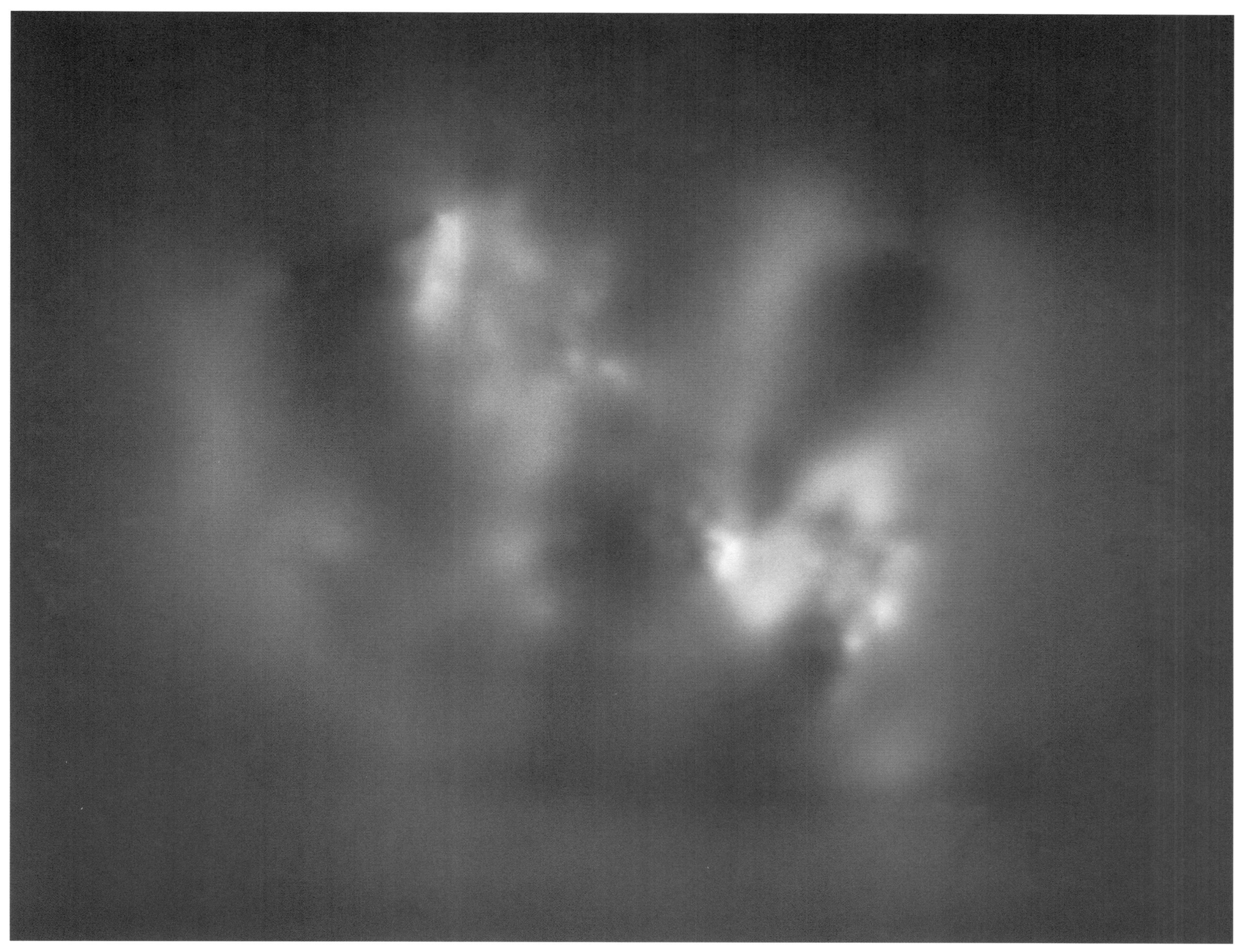

23. *Monticello, Utah,* 2001
Uranium autoradiograph

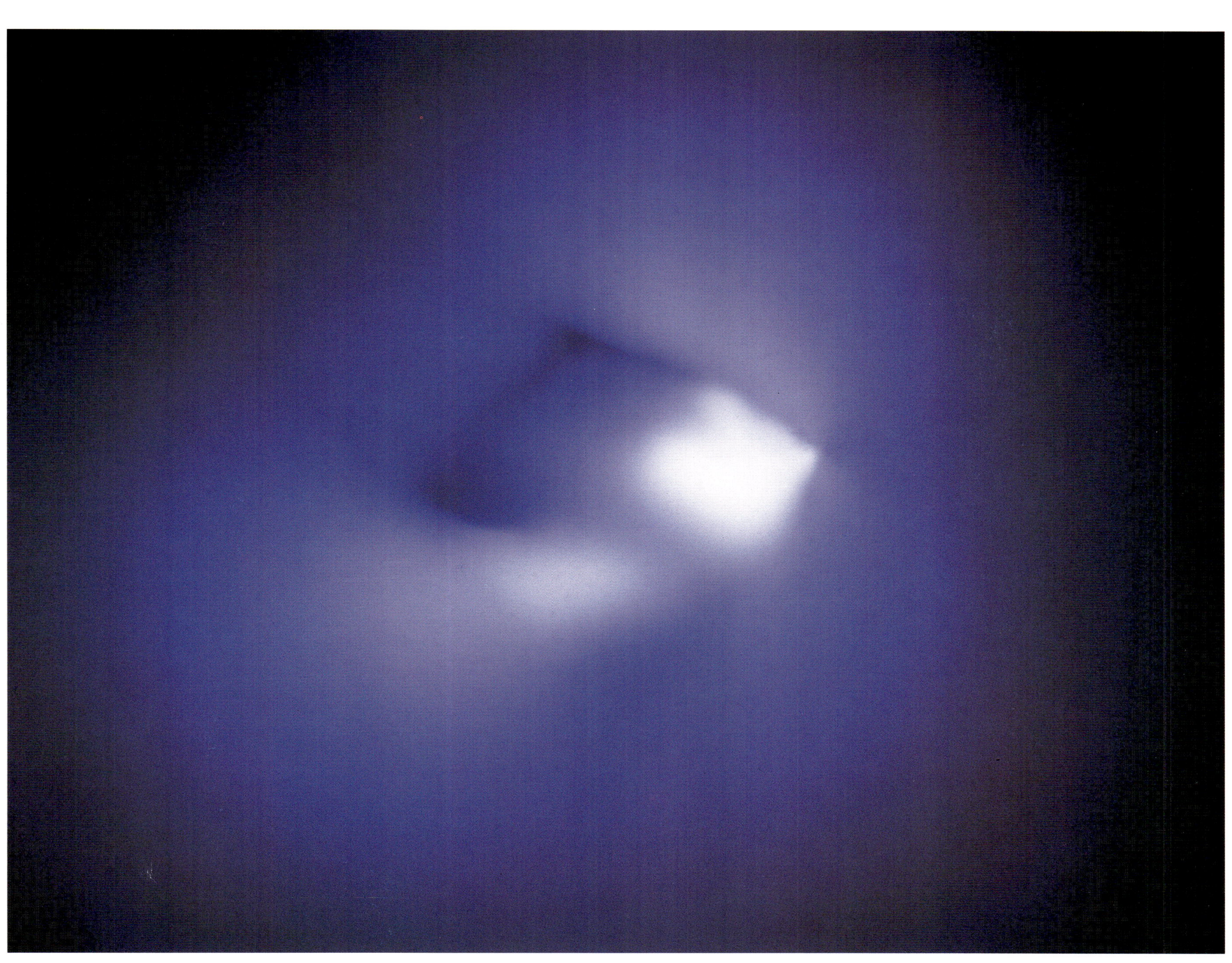

24. *Katanga, Congo,* 2001
Uranium autoradiograph

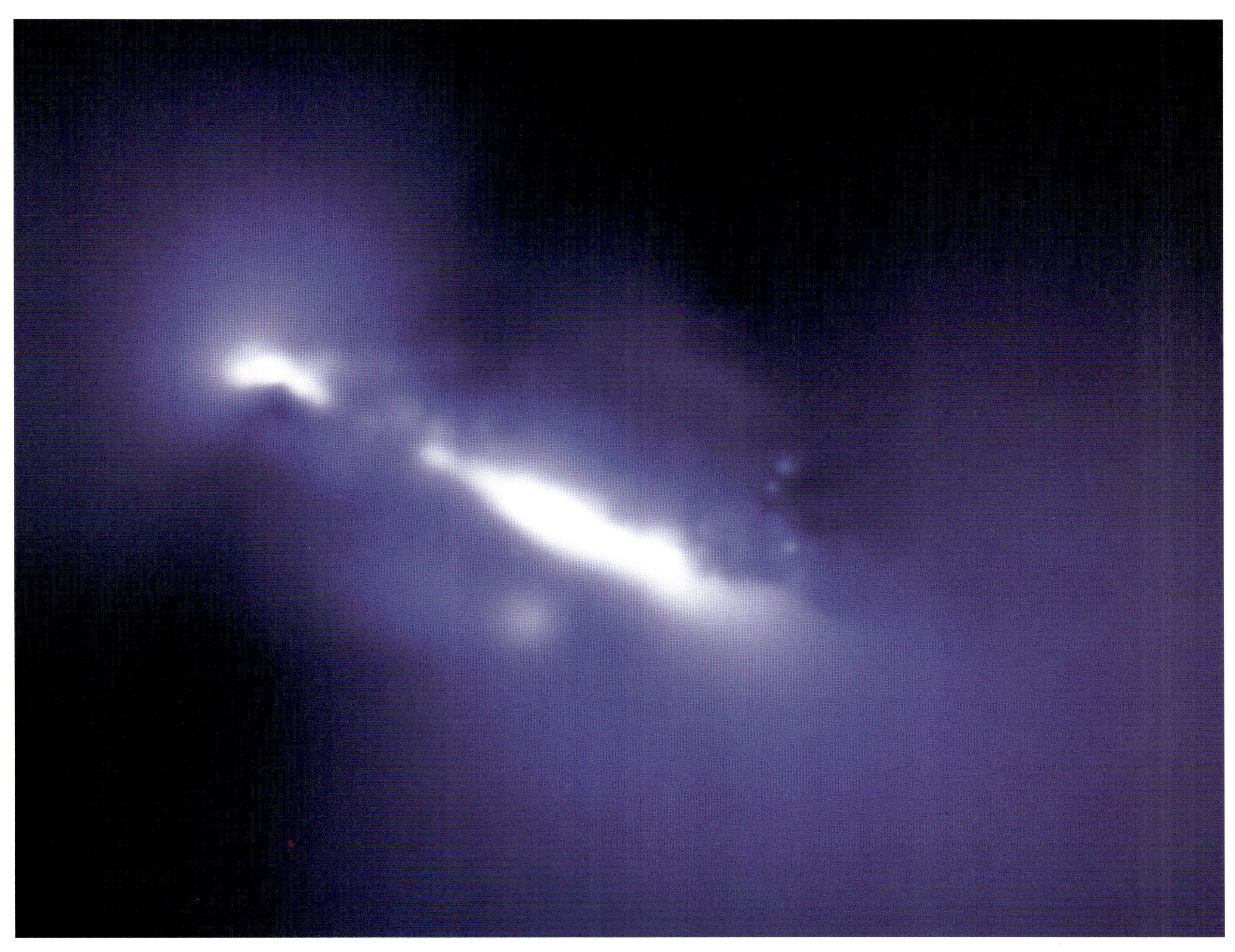

25. *Shinkolobwe, Congo,* 2001
Uranium autoradiograph

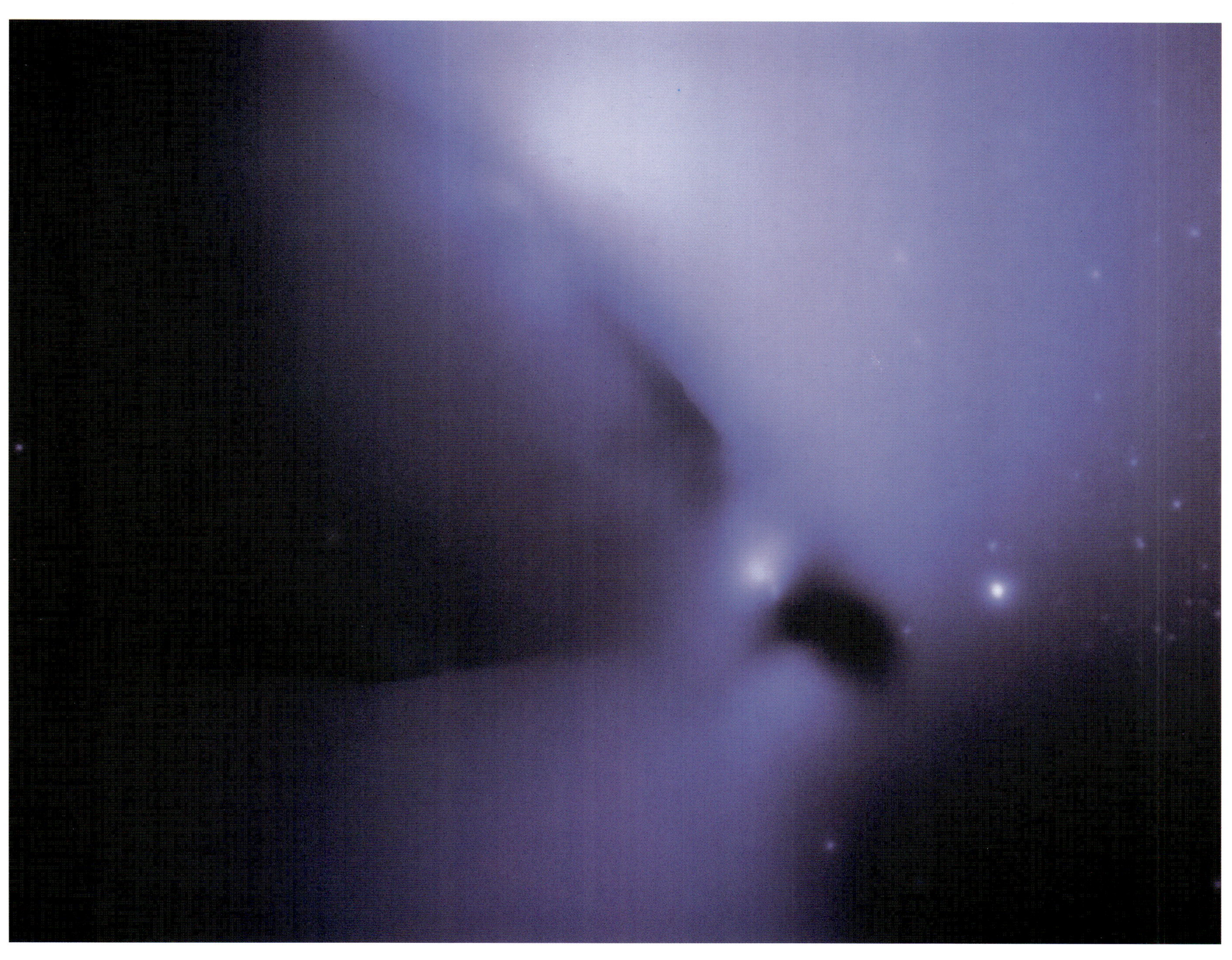

26. *Carrizozo, N.M., July 16, 1945,* 2002
Radium clock dial

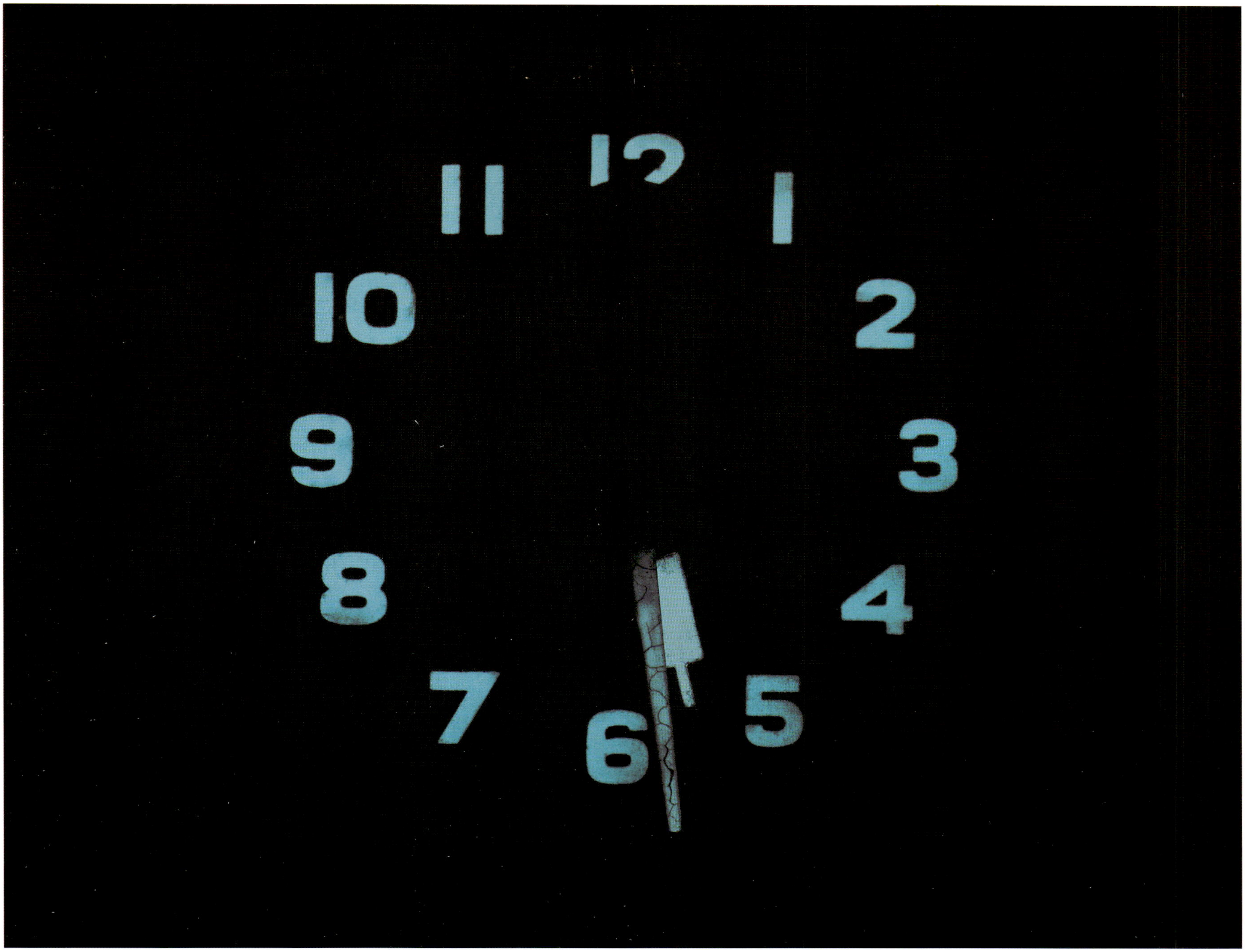

27. *Albuquerque, N.M., July 16, 1945,* 2001
Radium clock dial

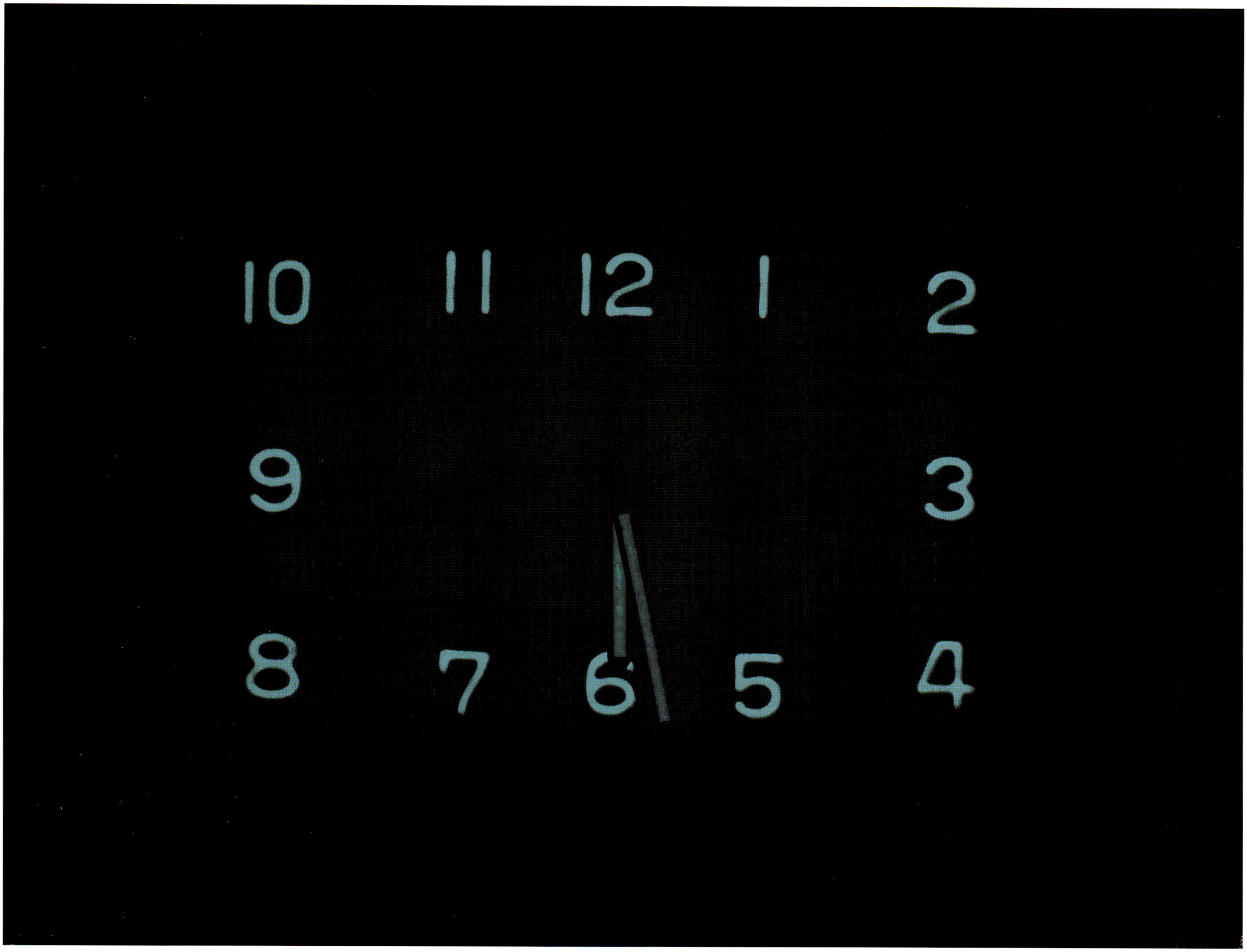

28. *Ancho, N.M., July 16, 1945,* 2001
Radium clock dial

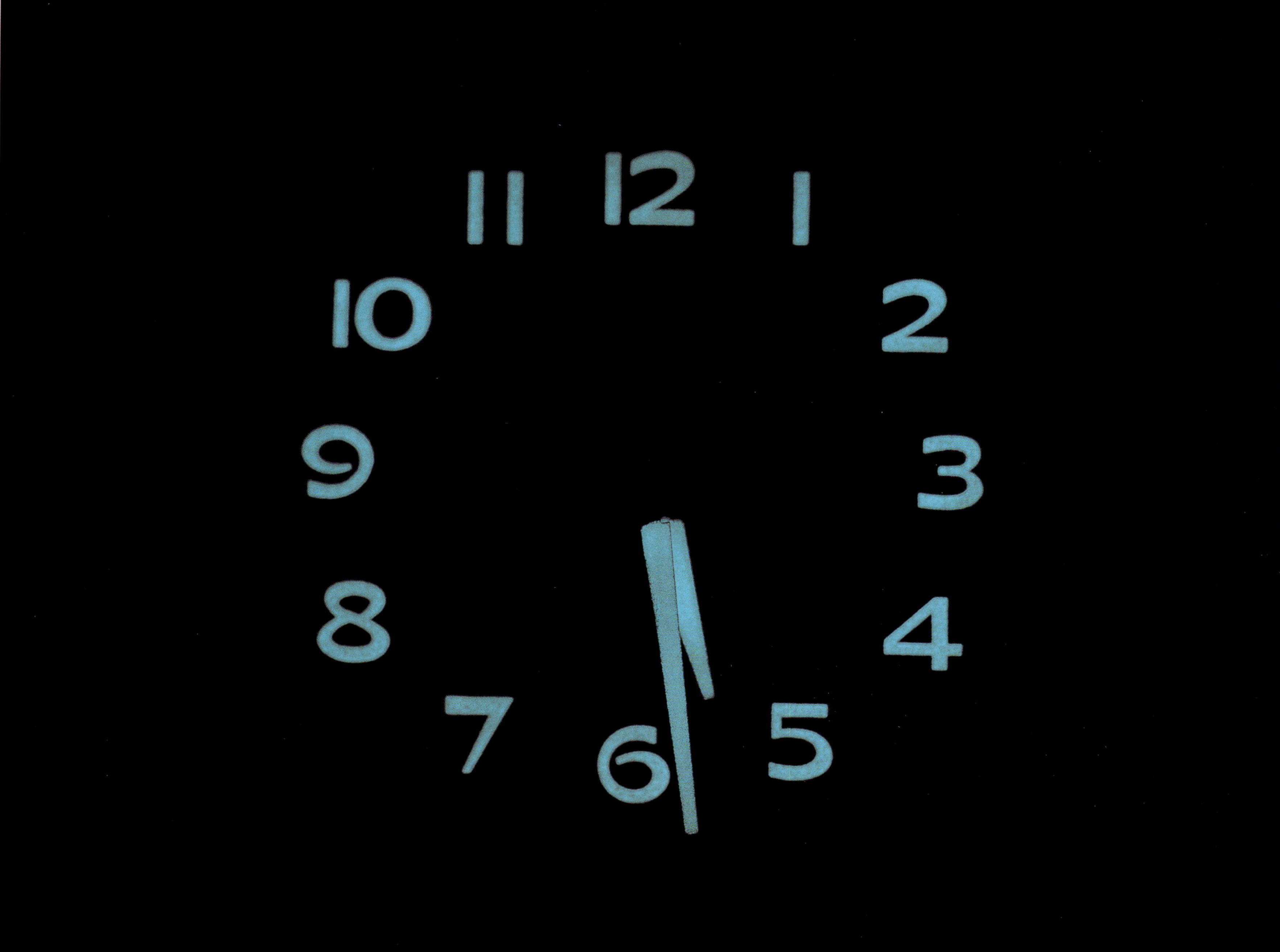

29. *Las Cruces, N.M., July 16, 1945,* 2001
Radium clock dial

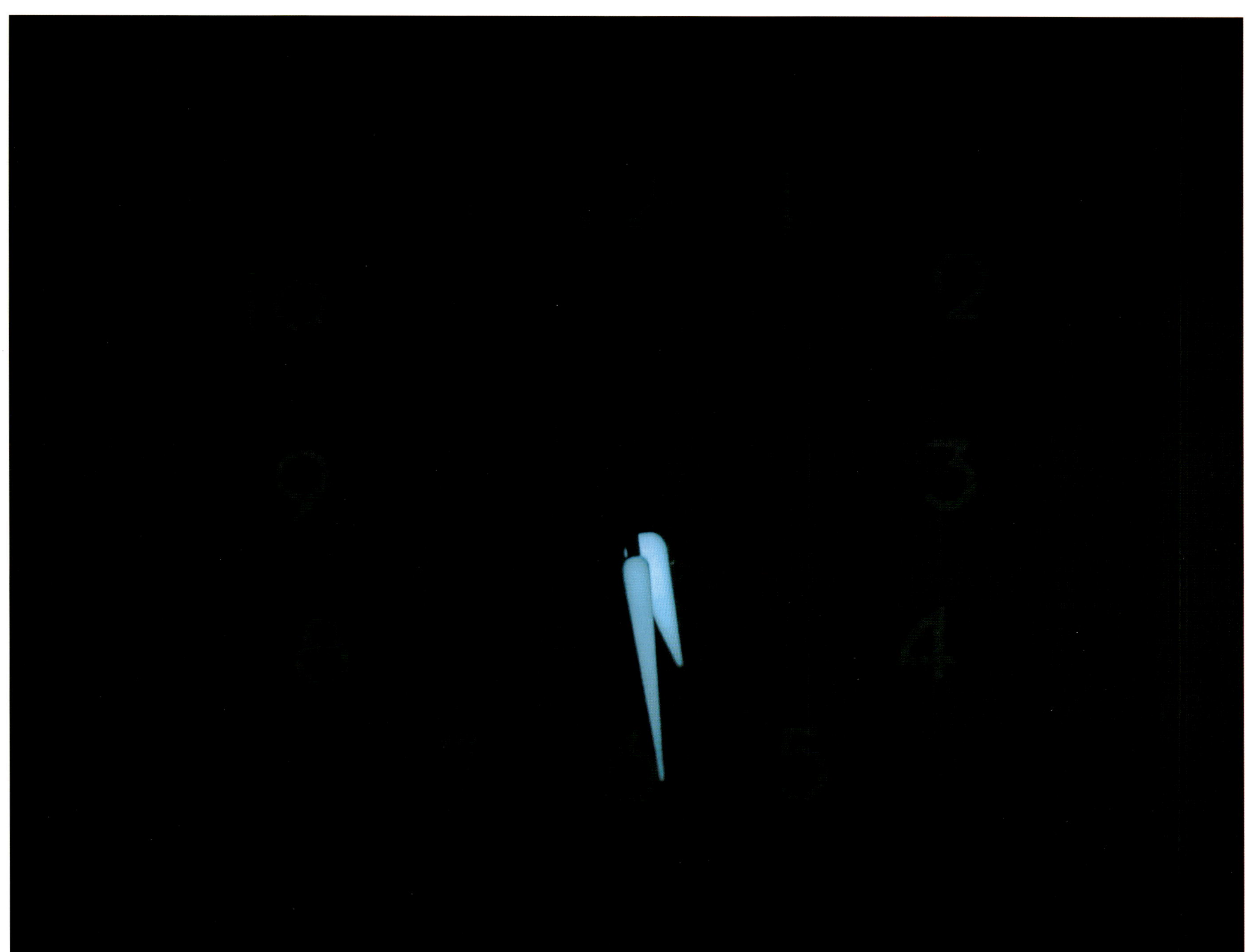

30. *Polvadera, N.M., July 16, 1945,* 2001
Radium clock dial

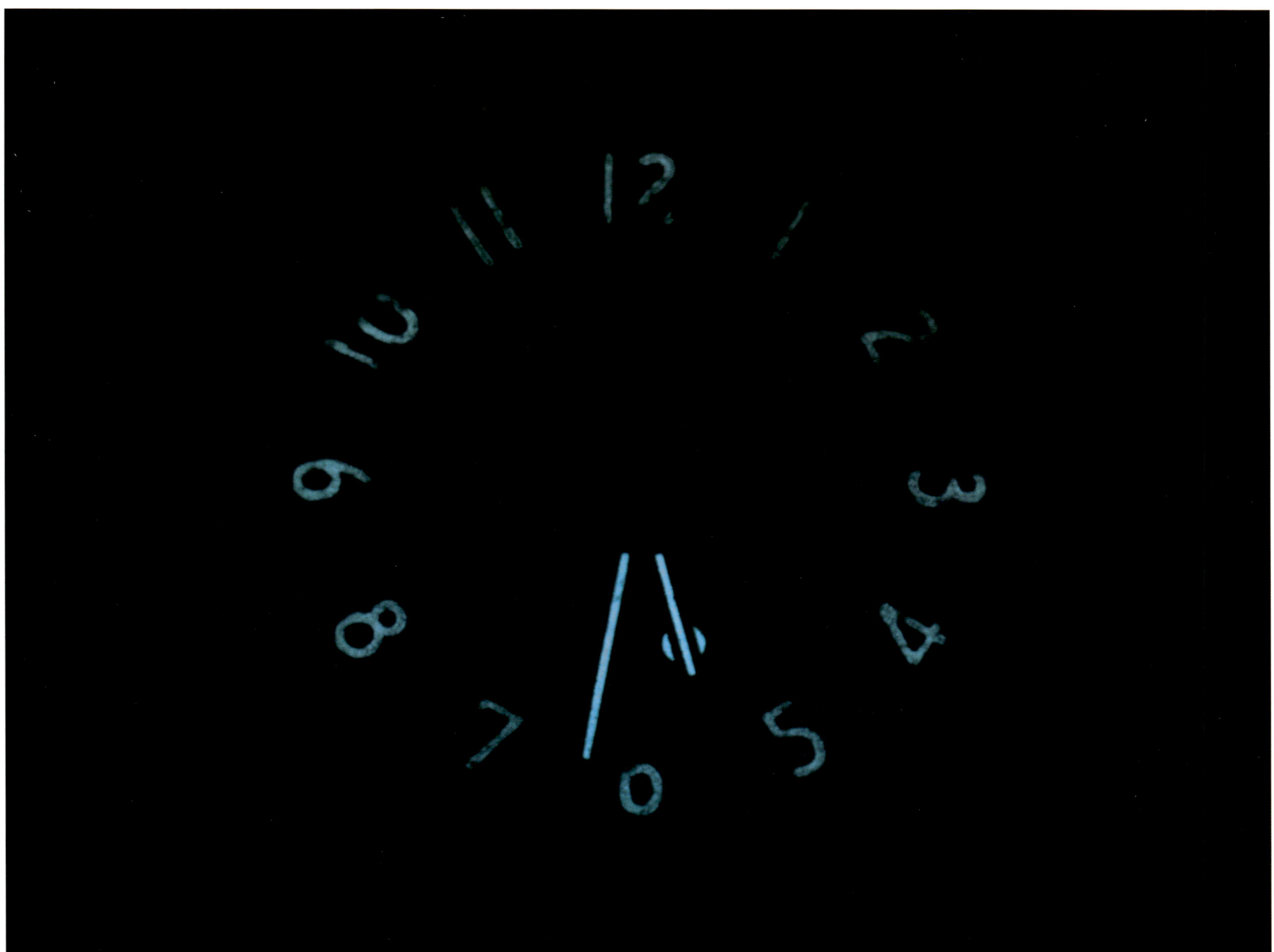

Materials, Process, and Meaning

An Interview with Jim Sanborn by Milena Kalinovska

Curator Milena Kalinovska's interview with Jim Sanborn discusses the artist's career from its beginnings in the early 1970s. The first section of the interview, titled "Primitive Science," deals with Sanborn's formative years and his fascination with the invisible forces of nature. The second section, "Science and Technology," examines the artist's first investigations into pure science, government influence, and their relationship to natural systems. The third section, "Big Science," is devoted to Sanborn's works in the Corcoran exhibition, Critical Assembly *and* Atomic Time. *The interview was conducted in Sanborn's studio in Washington, D.C., in January 2003. Unless otherwise stated, the illustrated works are by Jim Sanborn.*

Primitive Science

MK: Jim, *Critical Assembly* is the most complex work you have produced to date. It is aesthetically exquisite. It mesmerizes with its precise and beautiful electronics, hardware, and equipment, and yet conceptually it represents the most devastatingly direct critique of the use of atomic science. We cannot but think in your installation of the two atomic bombs that were dropped on Japan at the end of the Second World War, after which mankind entered a new stage in its destiny. Someone like the German artist Joseph Beuys was personally affected by war; he was a combat pilot for the German military and also taken prisoner during the war. His works continuously reflected on what it means to live the post-World War II experience. *The End of the Twentieth Century* consists of basalt stones, each with a carved circular shape, like an eye (fig. 31). These humanized stones are placed next to each other. Looking at the group, one cannot but be overcome by the ominous sense of how fragile human destiny is. Is Beuys someone you would consider a major catalyst of postwar art and of interest to you?

JS: I started doing my installation work after graduate school, in 1971. In the early 1970s I began to be familiar with Beuys's work. I found we did have tremendous similarities, in that we were both interested early on in science. I think he actually did a course in physics. I was very influenced by the natural sciences and had tremendous interest in archaeology and geology; these things also interested Beuys. Like Beuys, I employ natural objects and found objects and use them in large measure for their metaphorical content. For example, in 1983 I borrowed an Egyptian mummy from a university archaeology department and used it in an installation I did at the Virginia Museum of Fine Arts (fig. 32). I continued the practice of borrowing and exhibiting museum objects throughout my career.

My recent work is probably less metaphorical in nature than his. It is representative of itself, and more representative of big science than it is of primitive science, which Beuys was mostly interested in (fig. 33). To me, primitive science refers to the formative years of science, dealing with rocks and minerals and simple concepts of magnetism and electricity. Those things interested me until the mid-1980s. After that, the advent of big science in the 1940s, 1950s, and 1960s, when scientists began to build scientific monuments to themselves, redirected my focus. As far as social engagement is concerned, I think I do have a number of similarities with Beuys in that I do like to make commentaries on our social environment. For me, that environment changed. In the 1970s and early 1980s I was very interested in environmental issues. Sometime in the late 1980s I became concerned with the political and human ramifications of the U.S. government's international policies. I started delving into the difference between pure science and technological science. There is a very fine line between where pure science ends and technology takes over.

MK: Could you develop for us your initial ideas about environmental issues and how they related to your thinking about art?

JS: I was in the Pratt Institute M.F.A. program in New York from 1970 to 1971. In those years probably the most interesting work I had seen was Art Povera. Germano Celant's book *Art Povera* was published here in 1969. The galleries I frequented as a student showed some of the artists who were in the Art Povera movement, such as Gilberto Zorio, Giovanni Anselmo (fig. 34), Luciano Fabro, Jannis Kounellis. That work more or less opened me up. Art Povera seemed to make a lot of artists aware that the fields they work in may not be necessarily connected to the arts alone.

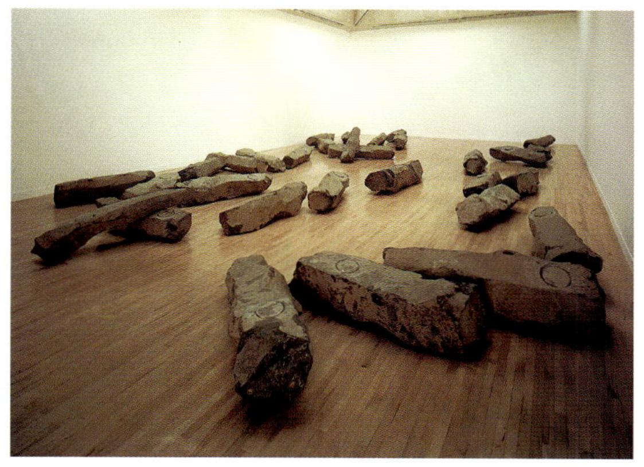

31. Joseph Beuys
The End of the Twentieth Century, 1983–85
Basalt, clay, and felt
Dimensions variable
©Tate, London 2003 ©2003 Artists Rights Society (ARS), New York/VG Bild-Kunst, Bonn

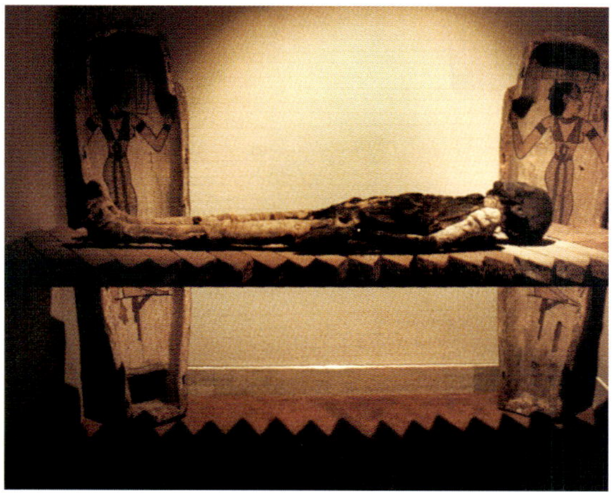

32. *The Mummy Room,* 1983
Sandstone and Egyptian mummy
7 x 10 x 4'
View of 1983 installation at the Virginia Museum of Fine Arts, Richmond

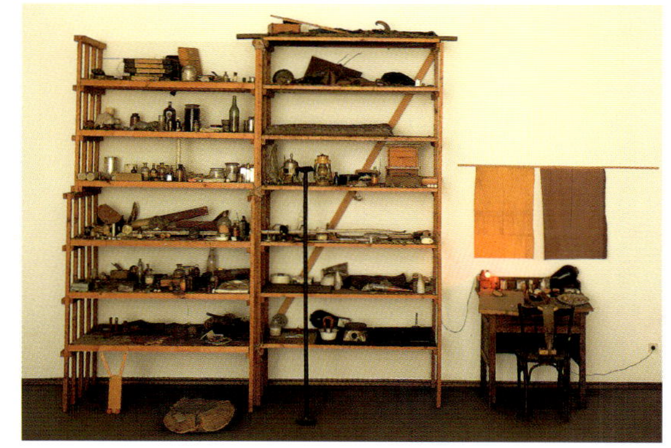

33. Joseph Beuys
Barraque d'Dull Odde, 1961–67
Mixed media
Dimensions variable
The Helga and Walter Lauffs Collection in the Kaiser Wilhelm Museum, Krefeld, Germany
©2003 Artists Rights Society (ARS), New York/VG Bild-Kunst, Bonn

Let's say an archaeologist or a physicist became interested in making art. A lot of the Art Povera work and, of course, Beuys's work allowed these people an artistic voice they didn't have before. I guess the thing that impressed me the most was the possibility of doing a body of work that was immensely personal, of not absorbing ideas from the outside but trying to absorb all the ideas that exist on the inside. I was interested in the environment. When I started out, archaeology and paleontology were my favorite subjects. In the process of digging in the ground for bones or artifacts, the ground itself became very important to me. Actually, my first university coursework was in anthropology and archaeology. So I went on a personal quest to find those things that I enjoyed doing the most. I felt as if I should, in my art, inform people of the workings of the earth, geological forces, really primal earth forces. I started doing work that was very descriptive of those sciences.

MK: Germano Celant stated that Art Povera tipped the scales between art and life toward the latter, an approach that marked your practice from the beginning.[1] Tell us about those beginnings.

JS: I began my environmental work in 1972. I used a friend's property in the country outside of Washington, D.C. In and around the lake on this property I did a series of ephemeral installations using man-made objects and others I had assembled and fabricated. Some floated in the water; others more or less dealt with the interface between where the land stopped and the water began. I was modifying the landscape in fairly minor ways (fig. 35).

MK: Were those first process-driven works shown outside of that landscape environment?

JS: Actually the first show was at the Virginia Museum of Fine Arts in Richmond in 1974. I used photographs of the environmental installations and also did a series of sculptures using hollow glass battery jars (fig. 36). These pieces sweated on the inside and responded to the environment. In the morning they would be clear glass, and in the evening they would be frosted, on the inside, by the humidity. So it was a whole series of works based on natural processes, where the glass would respond to temperature variations. Not long after that I did a commission in southern West Virginia. During the course of that commission I traveled back and forth on Interstate 77. At the time, I guess the late 1970s, this highway cut through mountain ranges in West Virginia, exposing the geological strata within those ranges. That particular highway project moved more earth than mankind had moved in its entire history up to that time. That was a point of pride with the West Virginia Highway Commission. But in excavating these huge mountain ranges, they had exposed the internal organs of the earth. I traveled back and forth on this highway seeing these internal organs and decided to build a body of work based on that.

MK: What was that body of work?

JS: They were stacked stone pieces that had various titles. One was called *Dormant Cone* (1979), and it, like the others, recalled glaciation, mountain building, plate tectonics, and all of those geoscience processes that were important to me at that time (fig. 37). Right after that I went into more cerebral work, which dealt with lodestone in particular. I was interested in the invisible processes of mountain building, such as pressure, tension, and time. Time in mountain building is a necessary quotient. Mountains are not built in weeks, months, or years. They are built in millennia and aeons. That kind of time we can't recognize, and so to us mountains are virtually motionless. I became very interested in the invisible forces of nature.

MK: Can you explain how these invisible forces were translated into materials you worked with?

JS: The first that comes to mind is magnetism, the earth's magnetic field and the Coriolis force, which result partly from the spinning of the earth (fig. 38). I did a series of works using lodestones, which I collected in fairly large quantities from a mountaintop in Utah (figs. 39 and 40). I found these lodestones by using a compass dial. The stones are naturally magnetized by lightning on the peaks of mountains. I found such a mountain within the boundaries of an iron mine. The mining company was in the process of mining the mountain and was ultimately going to destroy it. They gave me permission to pull these lodestones off the top.

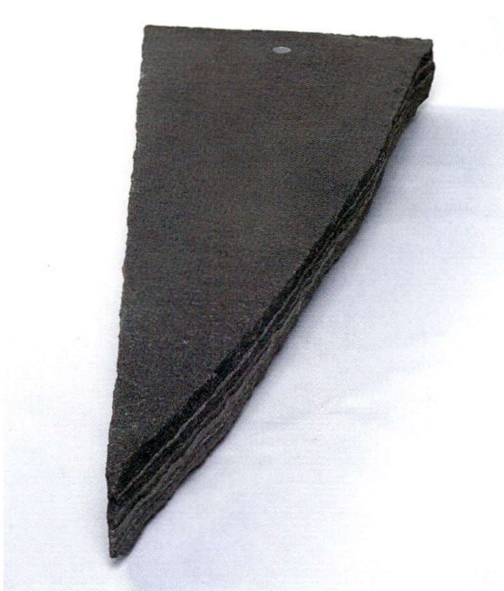

34. Giovanni Anselmo
Direzione (Direction), 1967–70
Schist, magnetic compass, and glass
6 1/4 x 70 1/4 x 27 1/2"
Collection Walker Art Center, Minneapolis,
The Frederick R. Weisman Collection of Art and the T. B. Walker Acquisition Fund, 1996

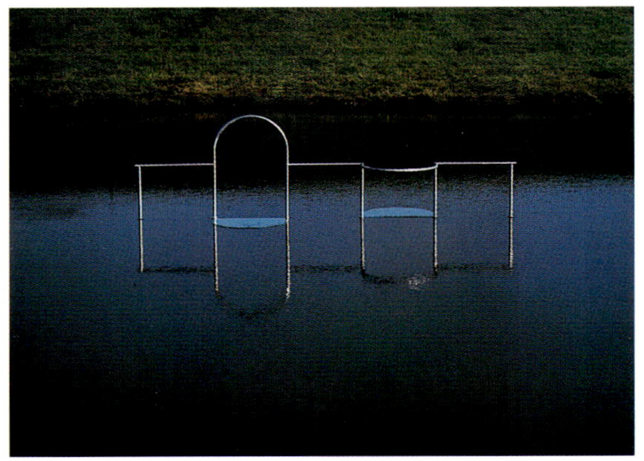

35. *Lake Piece*, 1972
Stainless steel and mirrored stainless steel
7 x 20 x 3'
View of 1972 installation at Howard County, Maryland

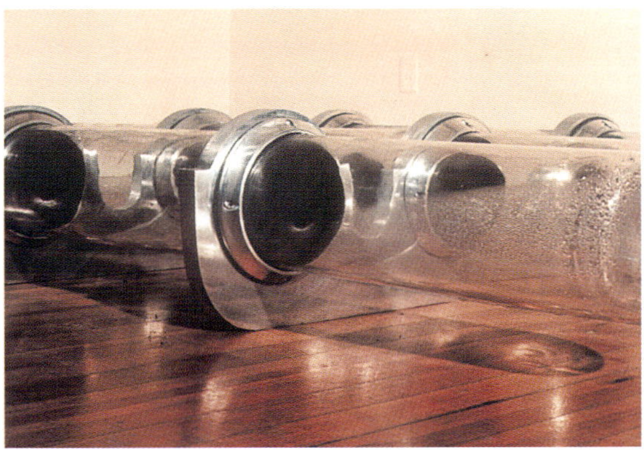

36. *Untitled* (Early Condensation Piece) (detail), 1974
Glass battery jars, aluminum, and water vapor
12 x 48 x 96"
View of 1974 installation at the Virginia Museum of Fine Arts, Richmond

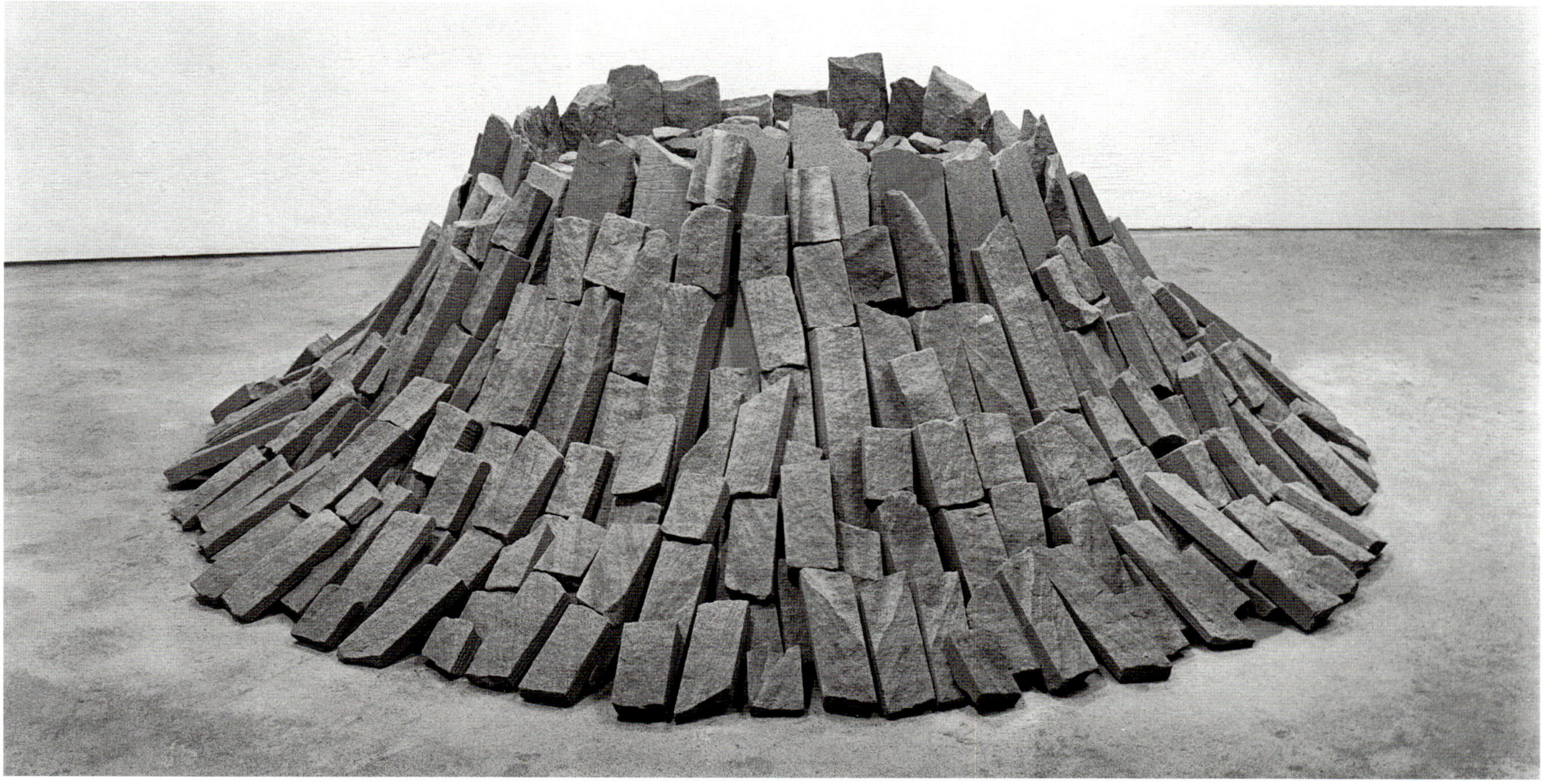

37. *Dormant Cone,* 1979
Sandstone
30 x 60 x 60"
View of 1979 installation at the artist's studio

I found the history of lodestones to be fascinating. As early as the Greek period, lodestones had been used for navigation. Electricity was more or less discovered based on work with lodestones. Before that, the Chinese had used lodestones for geomancy purposes, where they could spin a spoon made out of lodestone and more or less predict the future, using a lodestone pointer. I did a series of installations that made visible the earth's magnetic field. I made hundreds of compass needles, magnetized the needles, suspended them from a very fine line, and arranged them in large arrays so they would demonstrate the north/south position of the magnetic field of the earth. And juxtaposed with that, I would arrange the lodestones in such a way that I could deviate the earth's magnetic field. That demonstrated the power of the lodestone over the earth's magnetic field. This is actually an effect that challenges navigators all over the world. One piece I made, a tableau, was called *Lightning Horizon* (1983), which was shown in the exhibition *Content: A Contemporary Focus, 1974–1984,* at the Hirshhorn Museum and Sculpture Garden (fig.41). In addition, I did a series of installations in the early 1980s in which I used a lot of natural materials with reflective properties, meaning I could bounce light off of them. I did a series using mica because it is a great resister of heat, and light and heat are related (fig. 42). I used salt and saltwater (fig. 43). I used galena crystals and a lot of other geological materials, crystals, and natural substances (fig. 44).

Science and Technology

MK: Let's talk about how you moved from your environmental interests to focus on government and its political/international affairs.

JS: That happened about 1988. After working for eight years with invisible forces of the earth and nature, I decided to accept a commission from the General Services Administration for the Central Intelligence Agency headquarters in Langley, Virginia. I was chosen for the project because I had worked with invisible forces in the past, and the jurors felt that they were working with a commission for an agency that dealt with invisible forces, albeit man-made ones. This was an obvious philosophical stretch, but one thing did occur when I accepted the commission. I had some-

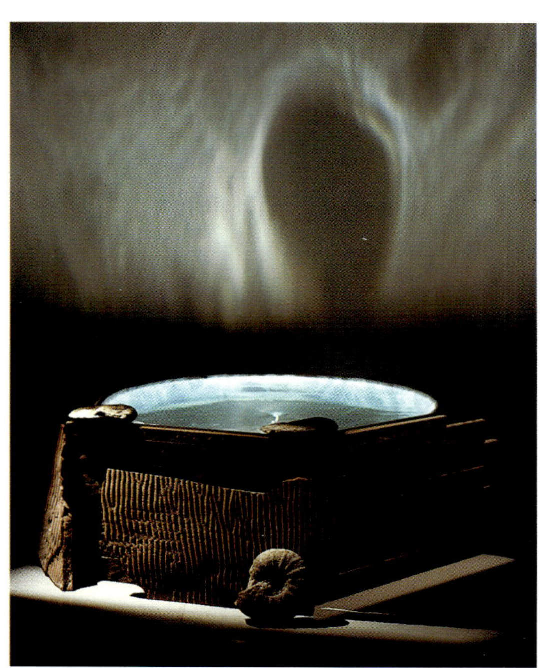

38. *Coriolis,* 1985
Fossil seabed, fossil shells, water, whirlpool, and light
25 x 25', dimensions variable
View of 1994 installation at the Phillips Collection, Washington, D.C.

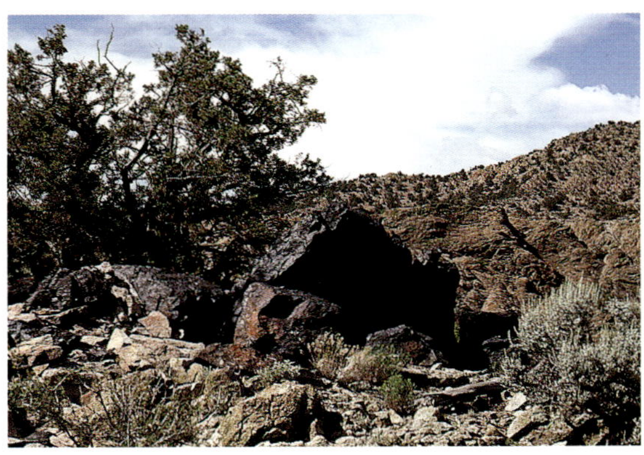

39. Lodestone outcropping, Cedar City, Utah, 1982

40. *Striking Stones under the Thunder,* 1985
Shadow, slate, sandstone, and lodestone
11 x 25 x 4'
View of 1986 installation at the Diane Brown Gallery, New York

thing of an epiphany in the research I did about the agency, actually the science of espionage. I realized there is a connection between the sciences and the invisible forces of man. I read widely on subjects as disparate as the mathematics of number theory, the algorithms of cryptography, the science of spying, the optics involved in satellite imagery, and the electronics in eavesdropping, and I realized that there is a very large scientific component to the work of espionage agencies. This was true for the KGB as well as the CIA.

MK: Could you describe the process of working on *Kryptos* (1988–90), the curved copper screen for the CIA inner courtyard and entrance, which you designed with plants, trees, pools of water, petrified trees, and lodestones (fig. 20).

JS: I have to preface this by saying that I was born in Washington, D.C., and I am very familiar with government agencies. In my first walk-through at the CIA I was stunned. They had built a new building, and it was still painted institutional green on the inside. I was very surprised that this building, which was supposed to be state of the art in 1990, still had a lot of the old governmental vestiges. The hallways were warrenlike for obvious security reasons. The windows were partially blocked, and a large part of it was underground. I decided to do the commission because I felt as if I might be able to make some sort of difference, in that I could work from the inside and somehow affect the thinking of the CIA. As naive as it seems, I attempted to do that. What I chose for the piece was to deal with the science of cryptography. Cryptography began in mathematics.

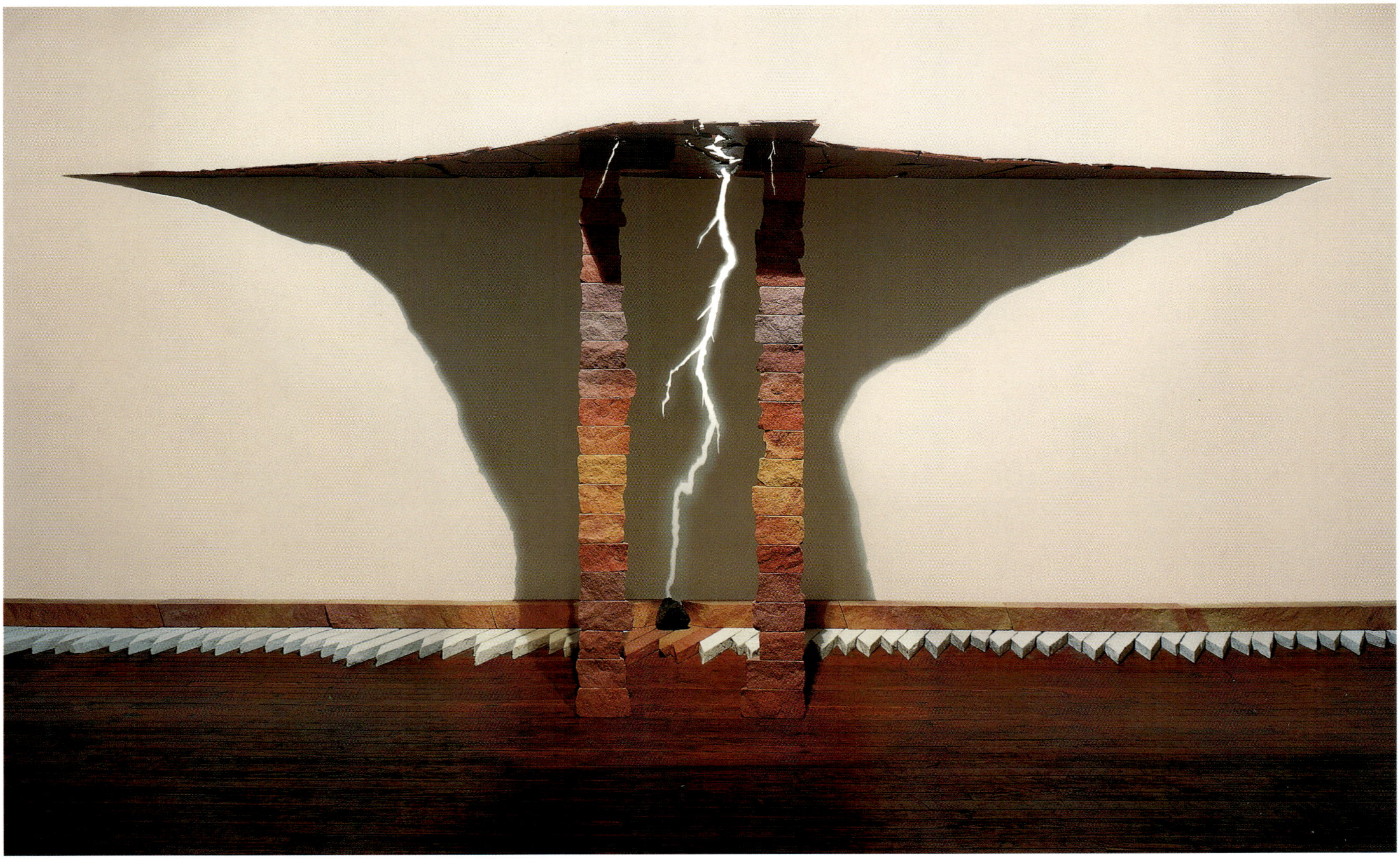

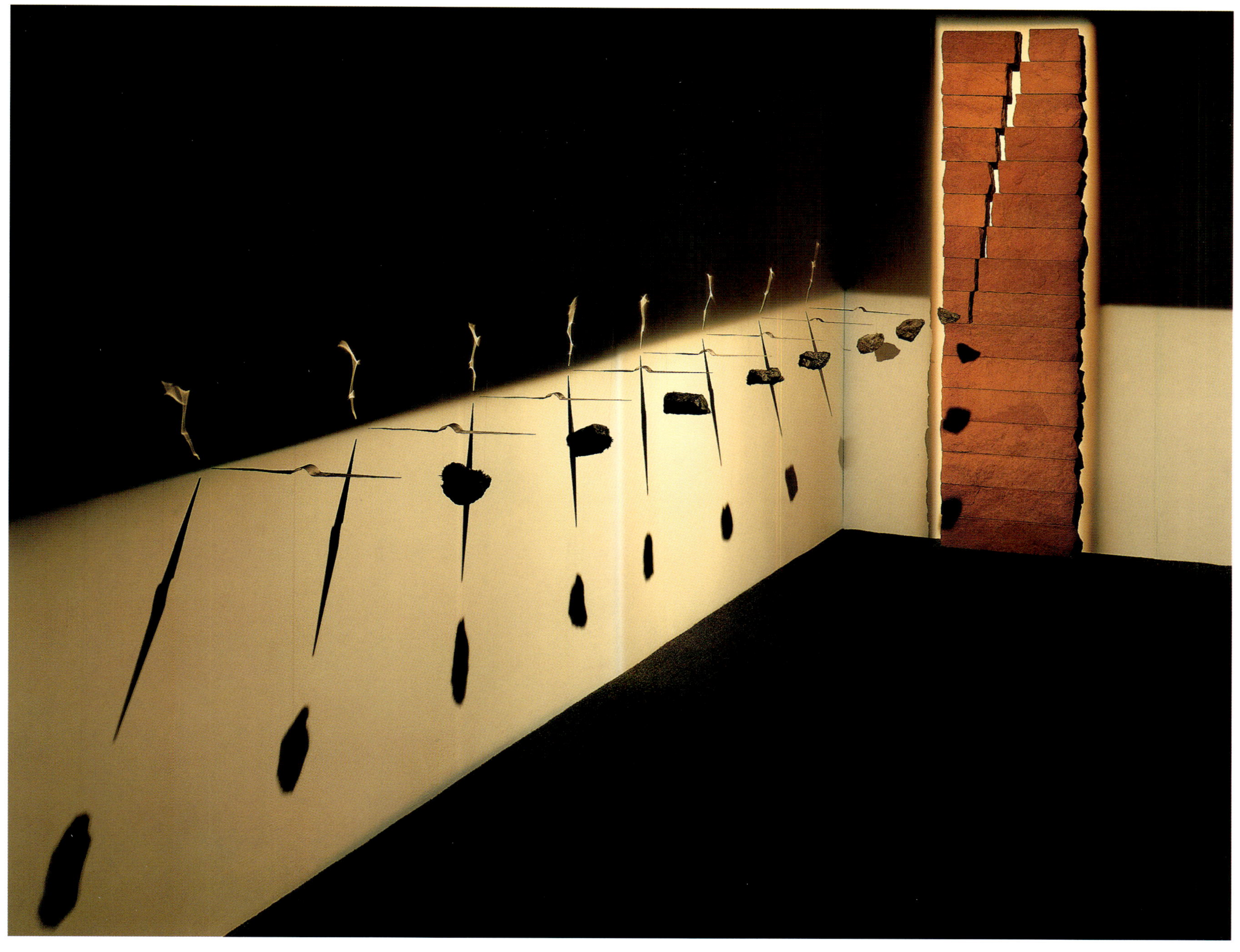

Codes were developed, even from Caesar's time, based on number theory and mathematical principles. I decided to use those principles and designed a work that is encoded. I wrote a fairly extensive text, then encoded it into a matrix system, which seemed to me, as an artist, to be fairly simple. I figured it would take the agency a year or two to decode, when, in fact, it took them almost eight years to get part of it. To date, they haven't cracked the other part. It ended up being something of a challenge for them to do. Physically the piece sits in the absolute center of the agency, in a courtyard, and perhaps it taunts them every day to think about something other than the documents they are working on at any given time.

MK: Since then, you must feel that merging politics with art is another way of communicating with the world.

JS: I adapted fairly quickly to that and discovered an underlying political motivation that I didn't know existed before that time. What affected me most profoundly was the realization that the sciences of cryptography and mathematics are very elegant pure sciences. I found that the ends for which these pure sciences are used are less elegant.

41. *Lightning Horizon,* 1983
Sandstone, lodestone, monofilament, and compasses
7 x 5 x 25'
View of 1984 installation at the Hirshhorn Museum and Sculpture Garden, Smithsonian Institution, Washington, D.C.

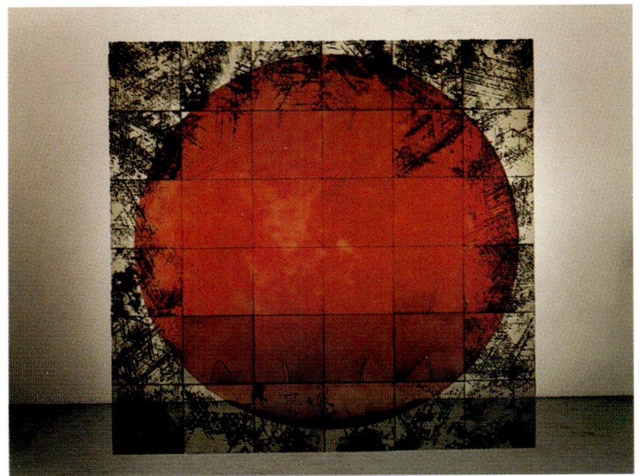

42. *Animisme* (detail), 1983
Shimenawa (rice straw rope), natural mica, 35mm film projection, monofilament, and stainless steel
6 x 6', dimensions of natural mica screen
View of 1994 installation at the High Museum of Art, Atlanta

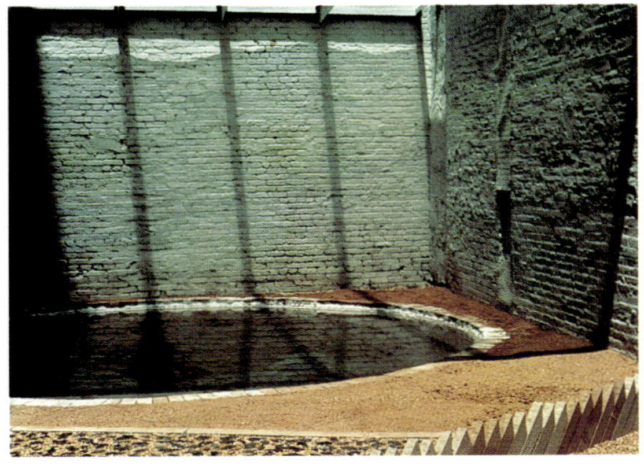

43. *Fire, Brimstone, and the Great Salt Lake,* 1982
Water, salt, mica, and copper
20 x 25 x 100'
View of 1982 installation in Washington, D.C., for the International Sculpture Conference

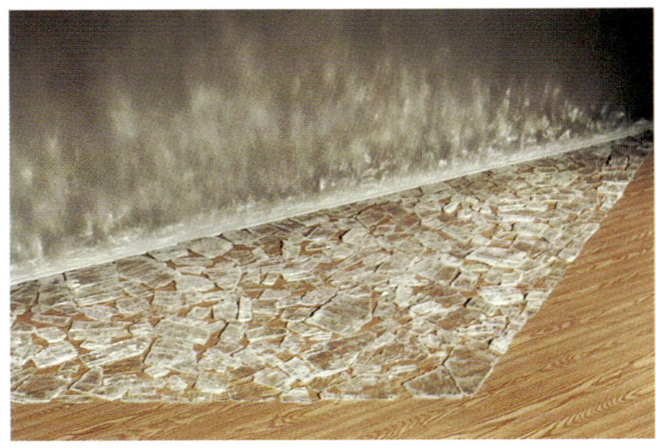

44. *Polar Horizon,* 1981
Gypsum crystals
4 x 10 x 4'
View of 1981 installation at the artist's studio

MK: Would you say that the CIA project and the experience associated with it led to your understanding that what is elegant, on the one hand, may not necessarily be so elegant from another point of view? Did the opposition of surface and content, of aesthetic surface hiding disturbing content, lead to other socially concerned projects during the 1990s?

JS: Yes. Within a year of doing the CIA commission, I did an exhibition at the Corcoran Gallery, in 1992, called *Covert Obsolescence*, which consisted of *The Code Room* and *The Listening Post* (figs. 45 and 46). From the titles you can see I was dealing with espionage in light of the Cold War. I saw the work of the agency as still reflecting a Cold War mentality, where the KGB versus the CIA was the big topic. But from about 1990 to today the topic has shifted tremendously. So now it's the CIA and Moussad versus Islamic radicals, et cetera. The Corcoran installation had some references to Greek mythology. There was a freestanding cylinder in the center of the room that was totally perforated with encoded text. Half of the cylinder was perforated text dealing with CIA operations. The other half of the cylinder dealt with KGB operations. The two existed side by side. A pinpoint light inside the cylinder projected these encoded texts, including the word Medusa, which was embedded in the texts, over the inside of the gallery, so that they covered every inch of its surface. It created an effect where Medusa's gaze, represented by these bright texts, fell over one's body as one walked through the room. There was a petrified tree in the room, a tree that had turned into stone. I felt as if the projected light was a visible ray that was as toxic as the information on that cylinder. It was a transformation from a text written to a text projected to a text that became toxic when it touched your body.

MK: Where did these texts come from?

JS: The text I chose was directly drawn from KGB and CIA documents that I had obtained from the Library of Congress and from a former KGB operative. One room was the projected text; the other room was the listening post. In the basements of embassies throughout the world and in Washington there are rooms that are covered with copper screen, and they are used for encoding and decoding incoming and outgoing messages. The code room that I used in the Corcoran installation was made entirely of pulped CIA documents that I obtained from the agency. Until 1991, the agency produced tons of these documents every day. They were destroyed at the end of each day and were taken from the agency in a pulped form. I made a deal with the director of Central Intelligence in which I gained access to this pulped material in exchange for offering part of the code of my CIA sculpture.

MK: What happened to your process-oriented projects after your espionage work ended in 1995?

JS: From 1995 to 1998, I did a series of installations in the western United States. I had to give my espionage work a rest as it had taken a lot out of me. I decided to do a series of projects in the environment. I returned to the western landscape and completed a series of large-format projections in remote areas. My original intention was to re-create in some way the work of the nineteenth-century cartographers and photographers who were hired to map and photograph the monumental western landscape.

MK: Had you done that kind of work before?

JS: The projection work began many years earlier in the installations using theatrical lighting and reflection.

MK: What was your rationale for this body of work?

JS: Dennis Oppenheim, Robert Smithson (fig. 47), James Turrell, and other artists were doing large-scale installations in the natural environment. Those projects affected the land tremendously, and not always with a pleasing effect on the environment. Bulldozers were brought onto the land, and the land itself was manipulated. I decided to counteract that in some way and still do very large outdoor installations. I had completed several in the early 1970s in which I placed objects in the

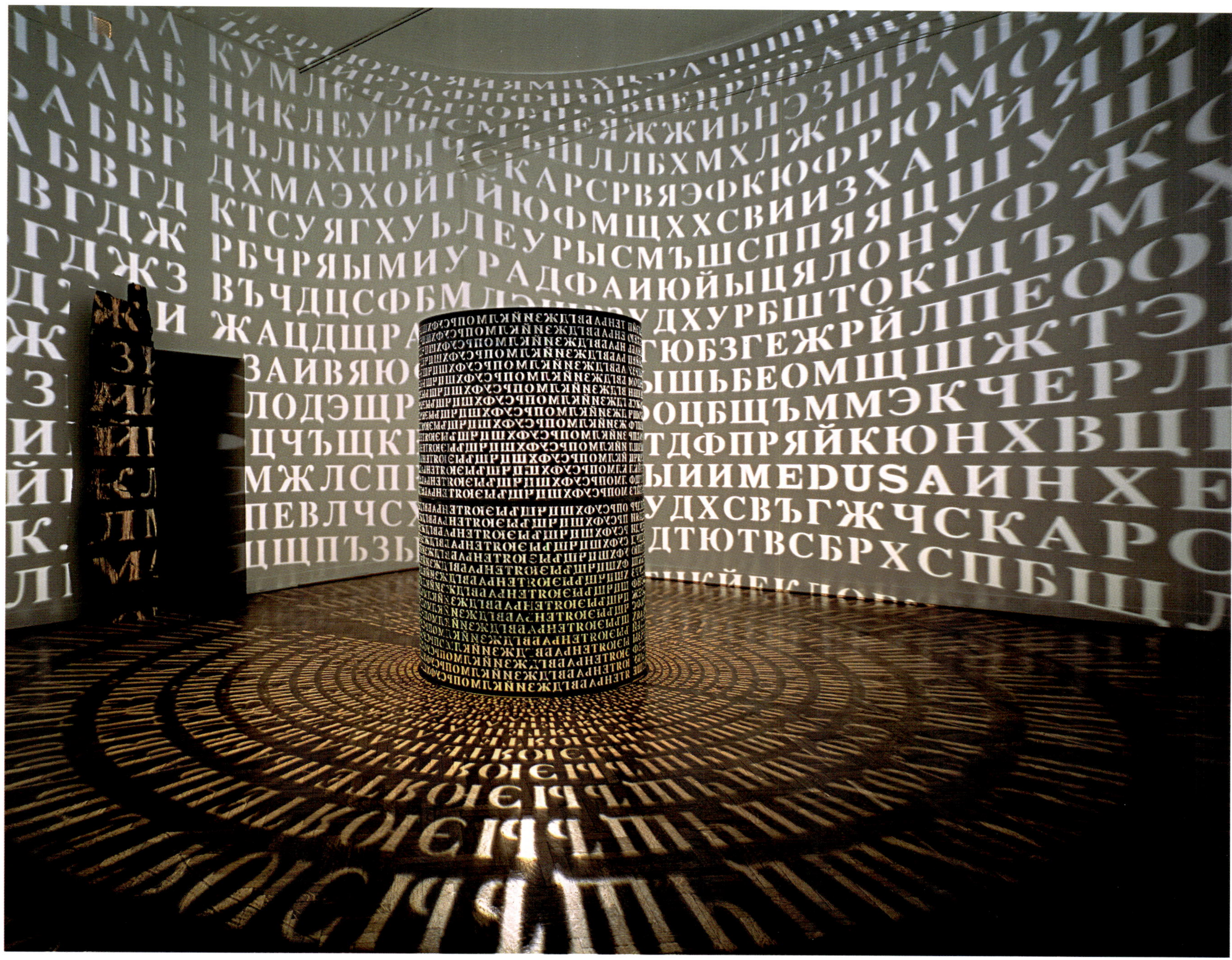

environment, and the end result was photographs of the outdoor installations.

MK: So what did you do this time?

JS: I learned to overpower natural daylight with large-format projections that I did for MIT in Cambridge in 1993 (fig. 48). The projector I used at MIT was very expensive, so for this project I ordered the lenses and some of the mechanical parts from Austria and built my own. I got a large generator and put this equipment in the back of my four-wheel-drive vehicle and drove into remote areas of the West to do some very large-scale projections. I began doing these projections by testing them from my studio in Washington. I was able to project gigantic images on a warehouse a quarter mile away. I practiced in the urban environment and then took it into the wilderness. I took a 4x5 camera with me, and the projector I designed was like a gigantic slide projector that used 10x10-inch slides. I worked with a typography company that generated maybe a hundred different transparency images that I had drawn. I designed these slide images based on Euclidean geometry.

45. *The Code Room*, 1992
Bronze cylinder, petrified tree, encoded text, and point-source light
19 x 25 x 40', dimensions variable
View of 1992 installation at the Corcoran Gallery of Art

46. *The Listening Post,* 1992
Copper screen, pulped CIA documents, 35mm film loop of lava falls, and theater lights
19 x 25 x 20'
View of 1992 installation at the Corcoran Gallery of Art

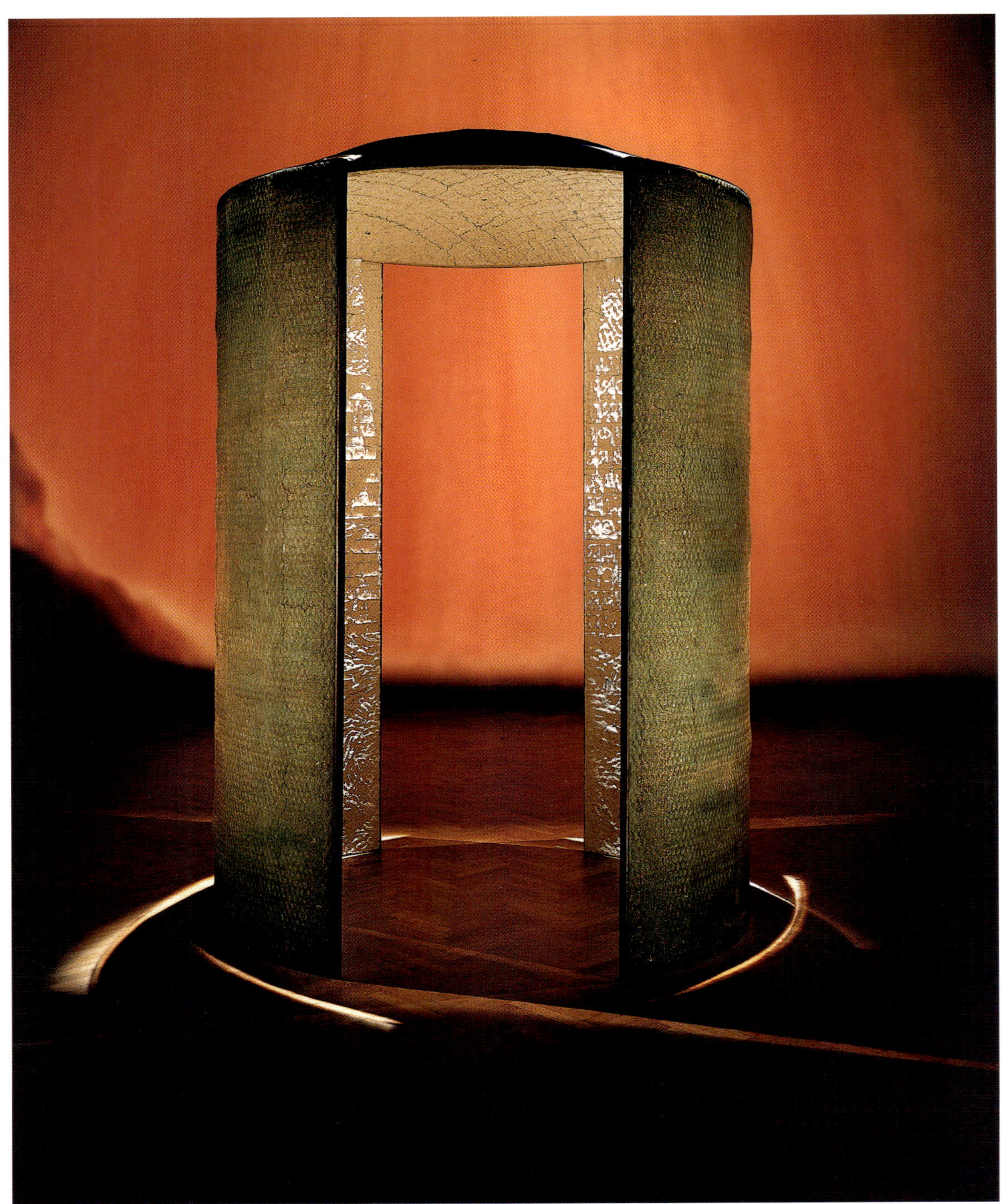

MK: How did you work?

JS: I had to choose remote sites so that I didn't get any lighting from cities or vehicles. The projections I was producing were so large and powerful that I knew they could be seen from miles away. I had to be in areas where I could work for five or six hours before anybody reached me (fig. 49). I was able to make images as wide as half a mile and have a very large impact on the environment without leaving a trace of what I had done. To me that was very important. I considered it a very gorgeous landscape, and I didn't want to muck it up. While it was amazing to be there doing these projections, it was basically only my assistant and I experiencing it. The only way I or anyone else could see those images again was by recording them on film, and I ended up making a series of Ilfachrome prints (figs. 50 and 51). I worked in the western environment every October from 1995 to 1998, except in 1997, when I went to Ireland (fig. 52). In Ireland I was part of a residency program called the Sirius Project. My base was Cork, and I traveled all over the country doing these projections as part of this residency.

Big Science

MK: Let's go back to *Critical Assembly*, which you began to work on after your projections. Before we go into the details of how you set about making it, I would like to talk about its political significance. In this context, another artist comes to mind—Hans Haacke and his politically charged installation *Germania*, which he did for the German Pavilion at the Venice Biennale in 1993 (figs. 53 and 54). Haacke is a German artist who has been living and working in New York since the 1960s. From early on, he has been interested in how everything is connected to everything else, and his installations, made in a variety of genres, are always critical in manner.[2] The construction of the German Pavilion was approved by Adolf Hitler and executed in 1938 to represent the new spirit and power of German art in the Third Reich. Since then, many artists chosen to exhibit in the German Pavilion have responded to the site in a variety of ways, and not just formally. Haacke worked with the site as a political place for art. He broke up the stone-slab floor. The central hall appeared vandalized, and above the wreckage was the sign Germania, appropriated from the front facade of the pavilion. At the entrance the artist placed a photograph of Hitler taken at the Venice Biennale in 1934, and above, in place of the Nazi eagle and swastika, Haacke installed a one-deutsche mark coin, the cash value of German identity. Jim, in *Critical Assembly* you have also decided to confront one of the most difficult, unresolved, and debated issues of World War II history and thus similarly bring into focus the relationship between art and political testimony.

JS: I think both Haacke and Beuys share with me an institutionalized guilt over the past of our respective nations. I find this kind of guilt disturbingly absent from a lot of American minds. I do find it present in a lot of physicists whom I have talked to about my project. There is some guilt about having designed an atomic weapon. Now as far as I am concerned, pure science is certainly guilt-free. When does the guilt start creeping in? The guilt starts when the pure science is sold, whether to a military or a commercial entity. I think there is a certain guilt in selling a potentially dangerous pure idea to anyone. The institutionalized guilt over the atomic program is definitely there. It was certainly there as soon as the flash was seen by Manhattan Project director Robert Oppenheimer, but it was felt much less by Edward Teller and some of the other hawks in the atomic program. The guilt touches a raw nerve. The rawness of that nerve, I think, needs to be tickled from time to time, or probed in order to bring up this discussion. It is not a discussion that anyone has talked about until recently. Before 1998, there was a hiatus and people placed discussions of the atomic program and atomic weapons on the back burner. Well, the reality is that since 9/11 we are in more danger from a nuclear weapon, far more danger, than we were in the Cold War. That is very problematic to me and should be very problematic to Americans in particular.

An artist's ability to make a political statement is one of the most fundamental forms of pure expression. I think the artist's pure expression is like the scientist's pure science. It is something that should be inviolable. There have been lots of contemporary artists, Chris Burden, Leon Golub, Nancy Spero, Hanne Darboven, Joseph Beuys, Hans Haacke, On Kawara (fig. 55), Gerhard Richter (fig. 56), and a variety of others who have been able to use this pure expression to make evident, clearly or between the lines, their political milieu. I am attempting by this installation to do a very similar thing.

MK: Each of On Kawara's date paintings, from his *Today Series* begun in 1966, is accompanied by a box within which is an actual document, a newspaper clipping from the day. This newspaper cutting contextualizes the painting in terms of the daily news and thus gives the entire work an unexpected political twist. Interestingly, Richter's paintings implicitly question whether the documentary medium can convey facts and thus fully record history.

JS: The documentary medium is subject to interpretation by the viewer and originally is subject to interpretation by the recorder. The artist adds a third level of interpretation. I agree with Richter completely and, like him, or like On Kawara, I am adding the third layer. I am personally adding sound and overall theatricality to my subject. I am also adding a layer of clarity by sharpening the focus of the image and its manifestation in the space. In other words, I am increasing sensory experience.

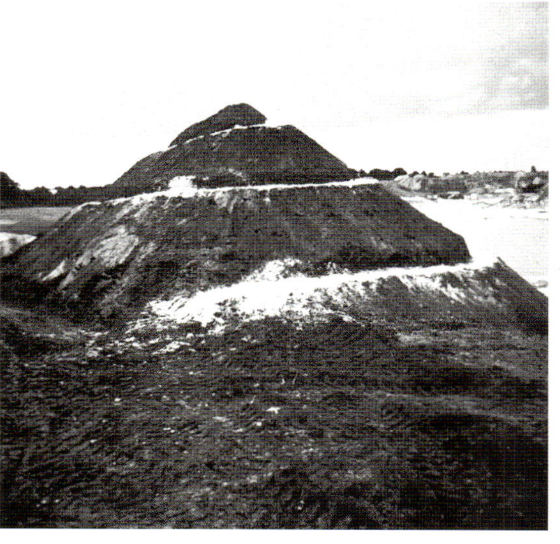

47. Robert Smithson
Spiral Hill, Emmen, Holland, 1971
Earth, black topsoil, and white sand
75' at base, approximately
Courtesy James Cohan Gallery, New York
©Estate of Robert Smithson/Licensed by VAGA, New York, NY

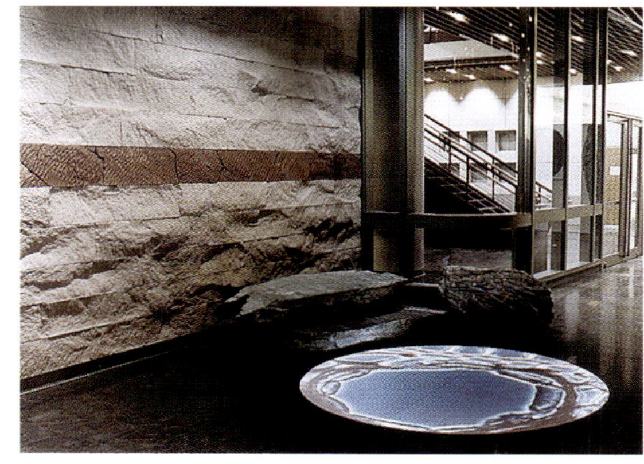

48. *Paleos* (detail), 1993
Limestone, fossilized seabed, petrified tree, slate, quartz, floor projection of interchangeable slide images, and modified Pani projector
13 x 60 x 12'
Collection of Massachusetts Institute of Technology, Cambridge, Department of Biology

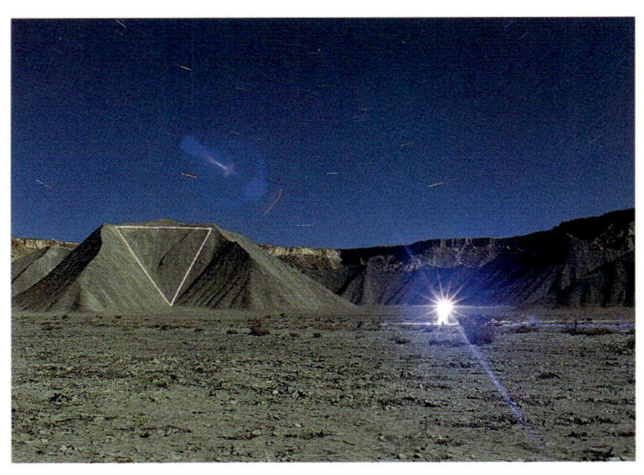

49. Jim Sanborn working in Horse Valley, Utah, October 1995

MK: You are bringing politics into art through the political object—the machines.

JS: Whereas Richter tends to be anthropomorphic in his subjects, I tend to use machines at face value. It is sort of a tyranny of the machines, the machines left on by mistake. Machines can take on a life of their own and end up with weighted symbolism, which can sometimes go beyond the human. I guess my machines are machines of power instead of people of power. I find that throughout my entire working life I have never really worked with the human form, except for the early Egyptian mummy piece. I represent a phenomenon, an invisible force, a psychological feeling, a terror, or something like that. I represent that mechanically in my machines. Lodestones and radioactive stones have a ponderous conceptual weight.

MK: What you are doing is calling on the viewer to complete the picture. You are providing a particular historical context for today's responsibility.

JS: Yes, I am sort of rebuilding the past. I am re-creating moments that bring to mind events in our past and things we have done that apply to the present and certainly to the future. Here I mean the genie that we released from the bottle in 1945 has come back to haunt us many times over during the last half century and continues to haunt us today.

MK: What about the tension in your work between aesthetics and ethics? Dave Hickey, an art critic and writer, in his four entertaining essays published under the collective title *The Invisible Dragon: Four Essays on Beauty*, debates current meaning as well as the role of beauty in the twentieth century. He argues against "the powers of patronage to neutralize the rhetorical force of contemporary images to minimize the slippage, as it were, between how it looks and what it means, because, as long as nothing but 'the beautiful' is rendered 'beautifully,' there is no friction and things do not change."[3] What you have done is use the beauty of execution to underline the horror of meaning.

JS: Yes, ugliness, a beastly quality.

MK: Is this something that disturbed you while you were working on this installation?

JS: Yes, to me this is the crux of the problem. Hickey's title is especially appropriate, as the Manhattan Project experiments were referred to largely as "tickling the dragon's tail." The dragon, here, is the immensity of nuclear power. The dragon comes up frequently in remarks that Oppenheimer made. The interesting thing is that the dragon image comes from East Asian cultural tradition. Dragons are beautiful things to behold, but they have deadly breath, among other things. I found that the beauty of the machines the scientists designed and built for the Manhattan Project were very seductive. In fact, the machines don't have to be as attractive as they are. Scientists work in environments that aren't necessarily always surrounded by beauty. Sometime in the 1940s there was an effort to start sprucing things up and make them prettier, and the Manhattan Project began to influence industrial design. For example, the designers began putting shining stainless-steel studs all over the dark matte faces of the electronics. In the process, all of these things were beautified, and the materials and concepts became gorgeous to the extent that they took on a design of their own. The scientists ended up building a sort of visual vernacular for the science. Big science began making fairly gorgeous and huge machines while maintaining great attention to visual detail. Every little gauge and dial and every little piece were polished and finished off. Even the Trinity device itself, the physics package in particular, was very gorgeous and jewel-like (figs. 7 and 8). There is a connection between engineering and the precise surfaces. It is an interesting relationship, where the more precise science gets, the more gorgeous it becomes, chaos theory notwithstanding.

MK: How long did it take you to build *Critical Assembly*? Is it a finished project now?

JS: The *Critical Assembly* installation itself seems to continually grow, modify, and change, as it isn't a set ensemble with a precise position for every part and every piece. It is a fluid kind of installation,

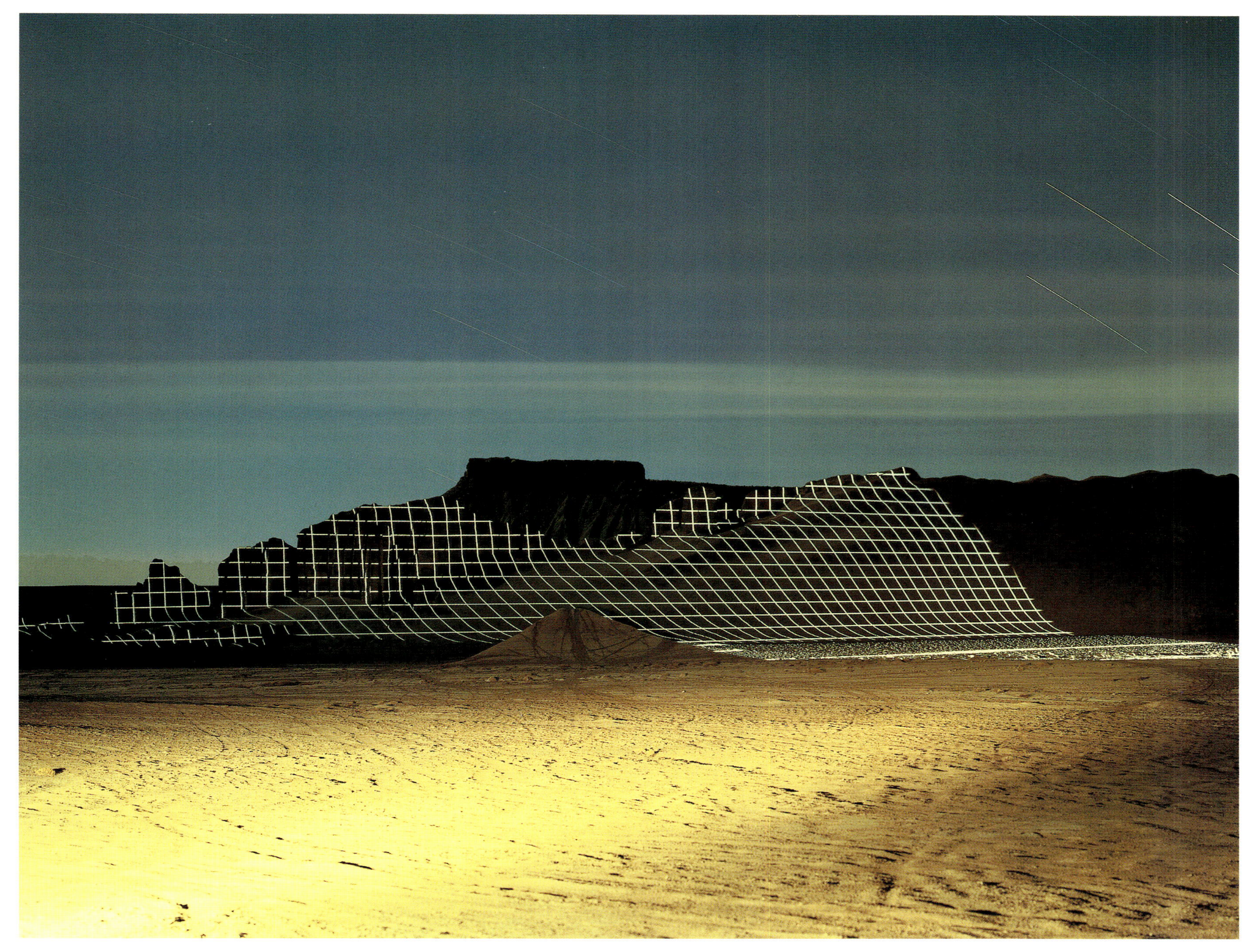

50. *110˚56'25"W 38˚22'22"N, Blue Mesa, Utah, II,*
1995
Cartographic projection
Large-format light projection, 400 x 1200 x 200'
Ilfachrome print
30 x 36"

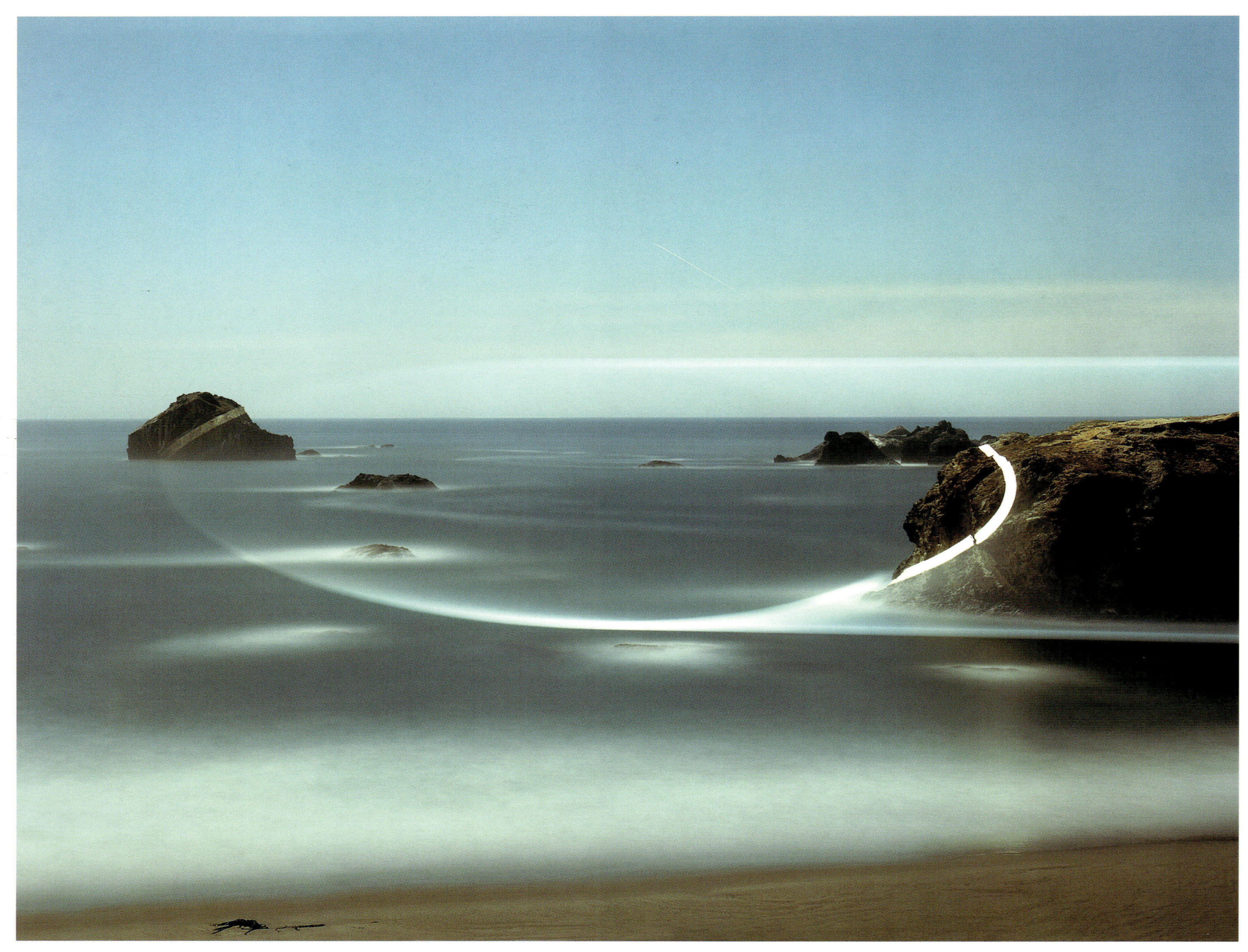

51. *Bandon, Oregon,* 1998
Light Volume Study 1
Large-format light projection into fog,
approximately 2 miles wide
Ilfachrome print
30 x 36"

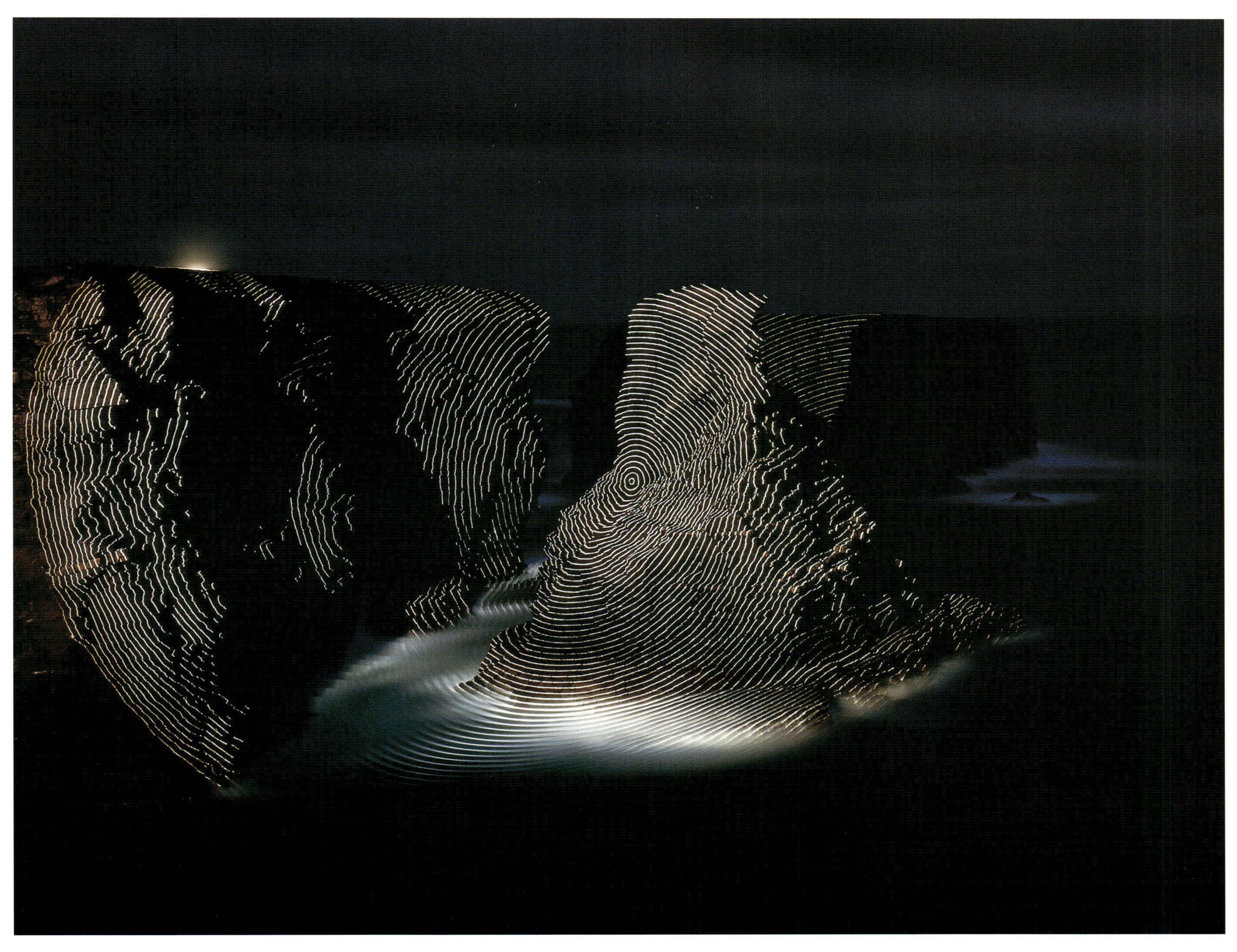

52. *Kilkee County Clare 1* (Ireland), 1997
Topographic projection
Large-format light projection, 800 x 1500 x 600'
Ilfachrome print
30 x 36"

much like science is a fluid thing. It will fit in many kinds of spaces. When I realized that I was going to re-create the laboratory of the Manhattan Project, I had to make a decision about how far I would go in representing something that is generally considered secret or classified. I decided to go as far as it felt comfortable to go. The problem is I never felt comfortable doing any of this work. The subject is so dour that it was difficult to work through. Filling up my car and trailer with all of the materials and equipment and bringing them back from Los Alamos was extremely difficult in itself. There was one night when I had to stay in a rest area and sleep all night long sandwiched in between the spheres that the bomb was made out of and the electronics that first controlled these things. It was very scary and spooky to be sandwiched in there. I didn't even know if the equipment was still radioactive. I had very interesting dreams.

MK: What were your thoughts during this period?

JS: Well, they were very depressing. The more I got into the project, the closer I got to the ethics of the subject. I worked on the actual re-creation of the Trinity device for about a year and a half, from 1998 to the end of 1999. It was a very dark period. The amount of research I had to do and the sources I had to use didn't exactly cheer up the process. While the resulting objects became shinier and more reflective and the lights of all the electronics lit up and got infinitely prettier, the subject didn't get any more benign. I was working on something that continued to get more technically beautiful, but the further I got into it, the subject got more and more ugly. The process resulted in my facing a serious conflict. I'm sure that the people who helped me do the work, the machinists and the companies that helped fabricate a lot of the parts, picked up on this because they asked questions such as, "What exactly are you doing?" I answered, "I'm re-creating the very first atomic bomb device." "That's very interesting." Everybody seemed interested, but everybody got a little depressed while working on it as well. It was a very intense process.

MK: How many parts would you say were fabricated for the installation?

JS: Oh, I don't know exactly. To make the device itself, about fifty parts had to be machined and very carefully assembled. I tried to use as much high-technology machining equipment as possible in order to speed up the process and make it affordable. I tried to do most of the work locally, but there were some things that required distant companies with expertise in making balls, for example. It is not an easy task to machine square materials into perfect spheres, and especially to machine cubic materials into spherical shells. Those kinds of machine tasks are difficult to accomplish. This is one reason atomic weapons are not easy for anyone to make. This was one of the challenges of the process, and it is very surprising that these challenges could be overcome in the 1940s using fairly primitive lathes, et cetera. Today it is all computerized, so it was much easier for me to do than it was for them in the 1940s.

MK: You also mentioned the different sources you had to rely on and read. Could you share some here?

JS: One of the first books I read was Richard Rhodes's *The Making of the Atomic Bomb*, which is really a fabulous work that describes the entire procedure, the reasons for and the process of building the first atomic bomb.[4] I contacted Rhodes's sources. A lot of his material came from a fellow named Chuck Hansen. His Web site is called the Swords of Armageddon. Chuck was an antinuclear activist who had the largest collection, outside the Soviet Union, of KGB material. He also had previously classified material from the U.S. government about weapons design, which he gleaned over many, many years of research. Unfortunately, Chuck recently passed away. I worked with KGB material and with declassified material from Los Alamos. A lot of declassified Los Alamos material has been reclassified since 9/11. In addition, I worked with technical papers and other material from the Internet, the major source being the antinuclear or nonviolence sites, and a lot of scientific journals.

MK: How did you come to develop, in relationship to *Critical Assembly*, a series of photographs you have entitled *Atomic Time* (figs. 21–30)?

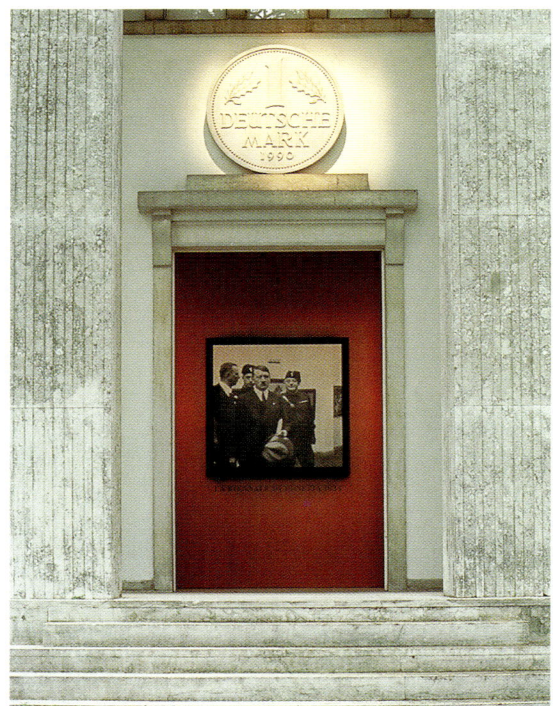

53. Hans Haacke
Germania (partial view), 1993
Installation at German Pavilion, Venice Biennale
©Hans Haacke/2003 Artists Rights Society (ARS), New York/VG Bild-Kunst, Bonn

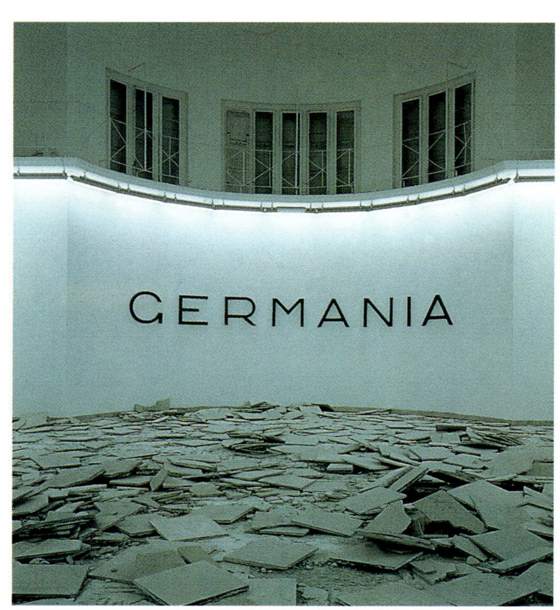

54. Hans Haacke
Germania (partial view), 1993
Interior of German Pavilion, Venice Biennale
©Hans Haacke/2003 Artists Rights Society (ARS), New York/VG Bild-Kunst, Bonn

JS: I came to *Critical Assembly* having already collected materials from around New Mexico, Arizona, and Utah for earlier projects. A lot of my early work used petrified trees, fossils, lodestones, and other materials that are prevalent in this region. Because materials such as these are exposed and lie on the surface in the Southwest, they are easy to get hold of. I had made many collections of various materials that have a conceptual weight and, I thought, because I was working on the bomb project, I should start working with uranium if I was going to be true to my subject. It was after I decided to work on the Manhattan Project re-creation that I began working with uranium.

MK: Were you concerned about the hazards of working with uranium?

JS: Obviously, uranium is a very toxic material. I didn't want to subject myself to radiation, so I used lead aprons, face masks, lead shielding, and all sorts of protective material and devices. There are lots of members of the scientific community who say it is relatively harmless. There are lots of members of the scientific community who say it is deadly. To be on the safe side, I was careful and collected very small samples.

MK: Where did you get the uranium?

JS: In the United States and Canada uranium mines are everywhere (fig. 57). But very few of those mines actually contributed material to the first atomic bomb. A lot of the material came from the Belgian Congo, and some of it came from Joachimsthal, in Bavaria. Actually the sources in Bavaria were some of the first that were used to discover the properties of nuclear materials. Marie Curie, the scientist who discovered radium, collected uranium samples from Joachimsthal, and Robert Oppenheimer, as a ten-year-old child, visited Joachimsthal and collected uranium for his own collection, long before he was in charge of the atomic bomb project. I set out trying to find sources for these materials and was able to get samples from Bavaria and Congo over the Internet. I got good advice from natural history museums. I also visited the National Atomic Museum in Albuquerque, New Mexico, and the Atomic Museum in Oak Ridge, Tennessee. In my early nuclear education I saw a couple of 8x10-inch images that were called autoradiographs. Marie Curie made a series of these autoradiographs. She took high-speed black-and-white film, placed uranium samples on top of it, and exposed it. They were called autoradiographs because, in effect, the uranium rock photographed itself, using its own radioactivity to expose the film. After doing a lot of research with a variety of photographic materials, I finally arrived at using 4x5-inch sheet film in ready-load packs. These are plastic packs that have film inside them. The uranium was strong enough—it had enough beta and gamma radiation—to penetrate the plastic package and to expose the film. It took between two and four weeks to make the exposure. I figured out how long an exposure was necessary through a process of exposing film, seeing if it worked, and reexposing it. It took months of practice to produce the images I wanted. Over a period of about a year and a half I made a series of these images (figs. 21–25). As I made the autoradiographs, I started collecting radium alarm clocks.

MK: Why?

JS: During my travels in southern New Mexico, where the bomb was exploded, I visited a lot of flea markets, as well as flea markets on the East Coast. I collected the clocks from the markets because I wanted to photograph the dials (figs. 26–30). The dials were painted with radium so they would glow in the dark. It was a very common practice that started about 1920. The radium-dial painters, as they were known, were young girls who painted these clock dials. They died by the thousands of very disfiguring cancers of the face and jaw because they licked their brushes in order to make the paint flow onto the clock dials a little more easily. I thought that these tragic events, and also the tragic event of the first atomic bomb blast, were all somehow related to the clocks. I envisioned the morning of July 16, 1945, at 5:30 a.m. in Alamogordo, New Mexico, where the first atomic bomb was exploded, and how, in the cities and small towns surrounding Alamogordo, there were radium-dial clocks on nightstands. When the bomb exploded at 5:30 a.m., it was still pitch-dark. The whole sky lit up as if it were dawn. A lot of people were awakened by this and the blast.

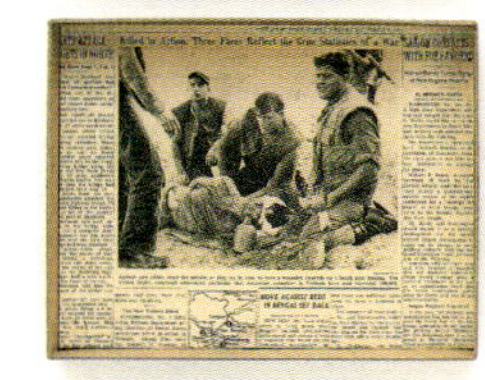

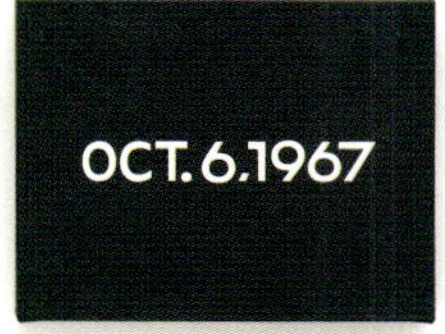

55. *On Kawara*
Oct. 6, 1967, 1967
Acrylic on canvas and cardboard box
Collection of the artist

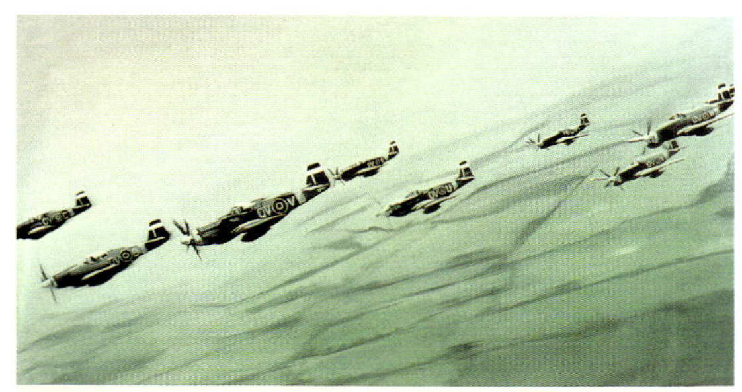

56. Gerhard Richter
Mustang-Staffel (Mustang Squadron), 1964
Oil on canvas
34 1/2 x 59 1/8"
The Robert Lehrman Art Trust

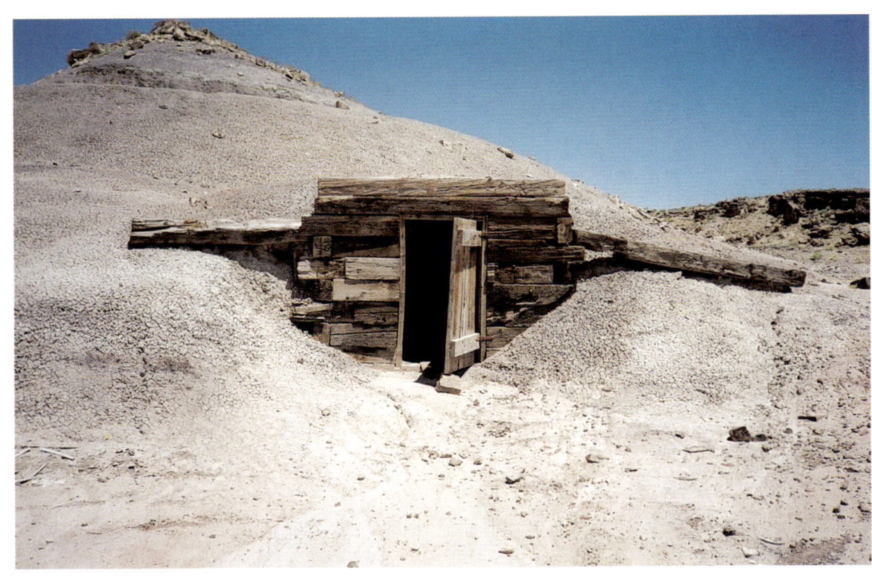

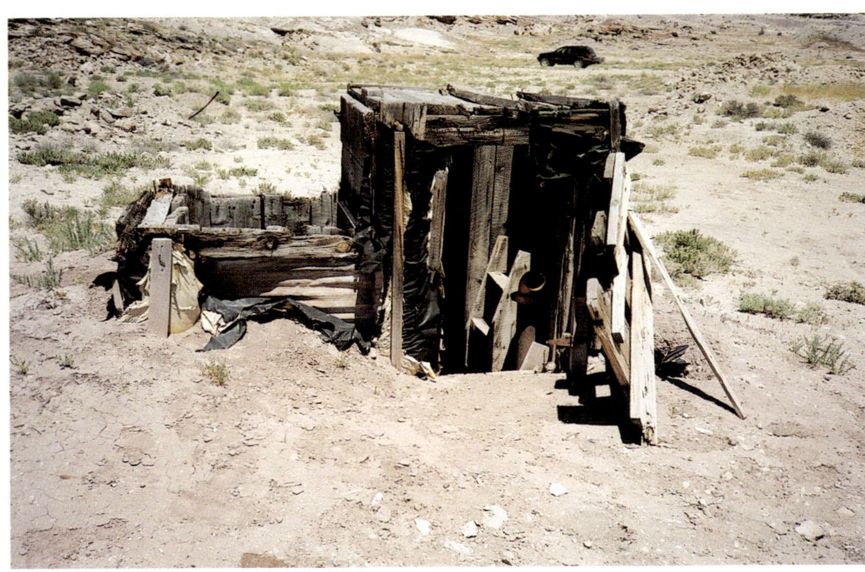

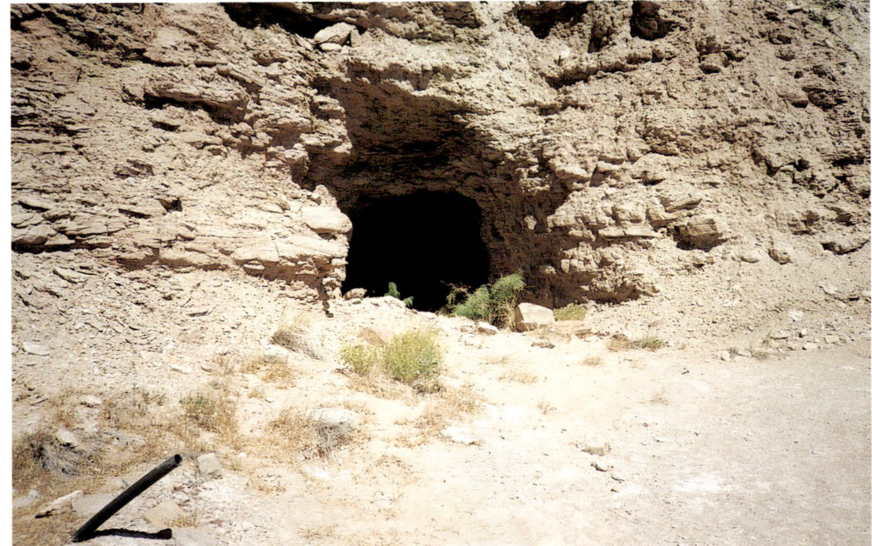

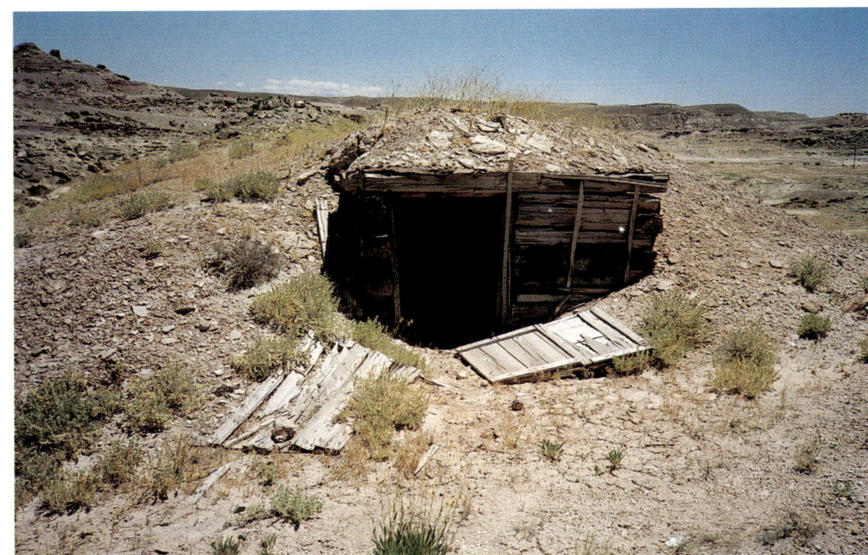

57. Four uranium mines near Green River, Utah, 2000

Bleary-eyed, they asked, "What happened?" And they looked at their glowing alarm clocks, which read 5:30, telling them it wasn't actually dawn yet. I thought it was ironic that it was radiation telling them what time it was and what time the bomb actually went off.

MK: How many of these clocks do you have?

JS: I have collected about twenty of them and probably every different style that exists. Every clock face is different. Some were made in Europe, but most were made in the United States. I went to the flea markets with a Geiger counter, so I could find which of the clocks were radioactive. I knew that those were the ones with radium dials. The problem is that the dials no longer glow at night. This is not because the radium is any less powerful but, rather, because the zinc sulfide that the radium was mixed with has degraded to such a point that it barely glows at all. I figured out that if I glued a clock down in a black box with a 4x5 camera with the shutter open, I could make a time-lapse photograph, a very long-term time-lapse photograph. With about a three-week exposure, the faintly glowing radium did make very strong images. Again, it was only through a very long process of trial and error and choosing the right film that I arrived at making the series of clock images. The clocks and the uranium autoradiographs constitute a series, which I call *Atomic Time*. Atomic time refers partly to the clocks I am using and partly to the way in which time today is measured by an atomic clock, which uses cesium. The most accurate time today is measured by radioactivity. Also, atomic time relates to the time in which we live. Considering how many difficulties and threats have been created by our letting the genie escape in the 1940s, I figured the title *Atomic Time* would be appropriate to cover the entire project.

MK: In a way this entire body of work is an antimonument to our time. Because of its human dimension, both conceptually and physically, it brings to mind other contemporary monuments such as the powerful Vietnam Veterans Memorial by Maya Lin (fig. 58).

JS: The power of the Vietnam Veterans Memorial is in how it brings humans into the picture and deals with the death of a large portion of humanity. My work is more or less a requiem for machines. My last show for the Corcoran, *Covert Obsolescence*, and the project I did for the Central Intelligence Agency were responses to the end of the Cold War. At that time I was making monuments to an obsolete tradecraft of the Cold War. What I am doing now is making something akin to a monument to an obsolete nuclear tradecraft. In both cases the tradecraft continues. The machines continue and the science continues and it continues to get us in trouble.

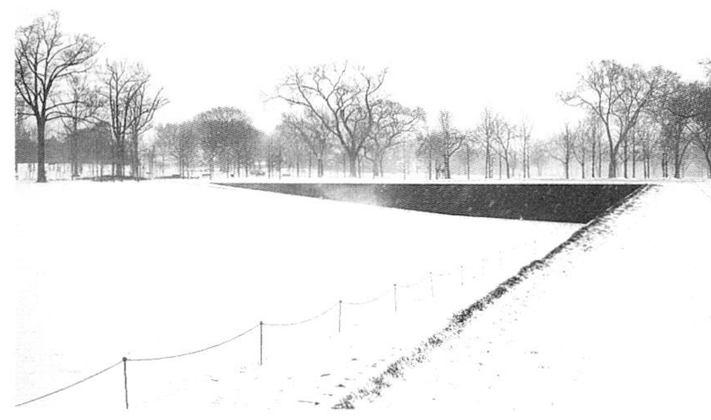

58. Maya Lin
Vietnam Veterans Memorial, 1982
Granite
Courtesy the artist

NOTES

1. Germano Celant, *Art Povera* (New York: Praeger, 1969), as quoted on the inside cover.

2. Klaus Busmann and Florian Matzner, *Hans Haacke: Bodenlos* (Stuttgart: Edition Cantz, 1993), 5.

3. Dave Hickey, *The Invisible Dragon: Four Essays on Beauty* (Los Angeles: Art Issues Press, 1993), 54–55.

4. Richard Rhodes, *The Making of the Atomic Bomb* (New York: Simon & Schuster, 1986).

EXHIBITION HISTORY

Born 1945, Washington, D.C., where Sanborn lives and works
B.A., 1968, Randolph-Macon College, Ashland, Va.
M.F.A., 1971, Pratt Institute, New York

SELECTED EXHIBITIONS

Solo

2003 *Atomic Time: Pure Science and Seduction*, Corcoran Gallery of Art, Washington, D.C.
Critical Assembly/Atomic Time, Numark Gallery, Washington, D.C.
1999 Numark Gallery, Washington, D.C.
1996 Grimaldis Gallery, Baltimore
1994 *Filter Media/Media Filter*, Nancy Drysdale Gallery, Washington, D.C.
1993 *Secrets Passed*, Orlando Museum of Fine Arts, Orlando, Fla.
1992 *Covert Obsolescence,* Corcoran Gallery of Art, Washington, D.C.
Nancy Drysdale Gallery, Washington, D.C.
1986 Diane Brown Gallery, New York
1982 Diane Brown Gallery, Washington, D.C.
1981 *US Projects*, Artists Space, New York
1980 Diane Brown Gallery, Washington, D.C.
1978 Virginia Museum of Fine Arts, Richmond
1977 Hood College, Frederick, Md.
1976 Washington Project for the Arts, Washington, D.C.
1974 Virginia Museum of Fine Arts, Richmond

Group

2001 *Between the Lines*, Kiang Gallery, Atlanta
The Altered Landscape, Scottsdale Museum of Fine Arts, Arizona
2000 *Landshapes*, Contemporary Arts Center of Virginia, Newport News
1999 Southeast Museum for Photography, Daytona Beach, Fla.
Altered Landscapes, Nevada Museum of Art, Reno
1997 *Public Art Biennial*, State University of New York at Purchase, Neuberger Museum
1995 Virginia Museum Fellowship Recipient, Peninsula Fine Arts Center, Newport News
1994 *Metaphysical Metaphors*, High Museum of Art, Atlanta
1992 *A Dialogue with Nature: Nine Contemporary Sculptors*, The Phillips Collection, Washington, D.C.
1991 Grimaldis Gallery, Baltimore
1988 *AVA 7*, Los Angeles County Museum of Art; Carnegie-Mellon Art Gallery, Pittsburgh; Virginia Museum of Fine Arts, Richmond
1987 *SECCA Ten-Year Anniversary Exhibition*, Winston-Salem, N.C.
1986 *Natural Settings,* Corcoran Gallery of Art, Washington, D.C.
1984 *Content: A Contemporary Focus, 1974–1984*, Hirshhorn Museum and Sculpture Garden, Smithsonian Institution, Washington, D.C.
Southeast VII, SECCA, Winston-Salem, N.C.
1983 Virginia Museum of Fine Arts, Richmond
1982 *Artists' Environments*, Maryland Institute College of Art, Baltimore
Diane Brown Gallery Artists, University of Virginia, Charlottesville
Washington Artists to Houston, University of Houston, Lawndale Annex
1980 *Forming Tomorrow Today*, Maryland Institute College of Art, Baltimore
International Sculpture Conference, Washington, D.C.
1979 *Selections*, Traveling Exhibition, Maryland Arts Council
Washington Project for the Arts, Washington, D.C.
Baltimore Museum of Art
1978 Corcoran Gallery of Art, Washington, D.C.
1977 Hood College, Frederick, Md.
Virginia Museum of Fine Arts, Richmond
Washington Project for the Arts, Washington, D.C.
1976 Baltimore Museum of Art
1974 Corcoran Gallery of Art, Washington, D.C.
1973 Virginia Museum of Fine Arts, Richmond

AWARDS AND GRANTS

1997 Sirius Project Residency, Cork, Ireland
1994 Virginia Commission on the Arts Grant
1992 Virginia Commission on the Arts Grant
Pollock-Krasner Foundation Grant
1991 Virginia Museum of Fine Arts Fellowship
1990 Art Matters, Inc. Grant
1988 Awards in the Visual Arts Grant
Louis Comfort Tiffany Foundation Grant
1986 Individual Artist's Fellowship, National Endowment for the Arts
1984 Artist's Fellowship, Virginia Commission on the Arts
1983 U.S. Representative, Kawasaki International Sculpture Symposium, Kawasaki, Japan
Artist's Fellowship, District of Columbia, Commission on the Arts
1982 Individual Artist's Fellowship, National Endowment for the Arts
NEA, SECCA Grant, Southeastern Center for Contemporary Art, Winston-Salem, N.C.
Maryland Arts Council Grant, Works in Progress
Individual Artist's Fellowship, National Endowment for the Arts

SELECTED BIBLIOGRAPHY

2000–2001

Dorsey, Catherine. "The Nature of Photography," *Portfolio Weekly*, 9 January 2001, 35.

Parker, Betty. "Sculptor Sheds New Light on Fort Myers," *The News-Press*, 6 April 2001, 1B, 2B.

Shaw-Eagle, Joanna. "Divergent Artistic Views Emerge as 'Group' at Numark," *Washington Times*, 15 July 2000, D1.

1990s

Beardsley, John. *Earthworks and Beyond: Contemporary Art in the Landscape.* New York: Abbeville Press, 1998, 176–78.

______. "Sculpting the Land." *Sculpture* (April 1996): 16–21.

Bell, Thomas. "Sculptor's Top-secret Mission: Improve Aesthetics at the CIA," *Washington Post*, 14 January 1990, C1.

Bostock, Cliff. "The Artist as Alchemist," *PARADIGMS*, 23 April 1994, 23, 25, 27.

Clements, Paul. "The Sanborn File." *Museum and Arts Washington* (March–April 1991): 40–41, 65.

Cullum, Jerry. "Art at the Edge: Metaphysical Metaphors," *Atlanta Journal-Constitution*, 22 April 1994, 11.

Dorsey, John. "Sanborn's New Geometry Highlights Natural Beauty," *Baltimore Sun*, 5 December 1996, 8E.

Ellis, David. "The Spooks' Secret Sculpture Garden," *Time*, 18 March 1991, 15.

Fleming, Lee. "The Shadow Shows," *Washington Post*, 1 October 1994, H2.

Forgey, Benjamin. "A Hand, a Wave, a Winner, 'Coastline' at N.O.A.A," *Washington Post*, 20 November 1993, B1.

Friis-Hansen, Dana. "Art in the Workplace." *Design Magazine* (June 1994): 35.

Gertz, Bill. "Cryptic Sculpture Spooks C.I.A. Employees," *Washington Times*, 8 April 1991, D1.

Gilbert, Chris. "Jim Sanborn." *New Art Examiner* (June 1999): 49.

Howe, Eleanor. "The Art of Public Art." *Popular Government* (Summer 1999): 2–7.

Hughes, Collin. "Secret Message of the CIA's $250,000 Sculpture," *Independent* (London), 17 January 1990, 1.

"Jim Sanborn's Coastline." *Sculpture* (July–August 1994): 40.

Johnson, Linda L. *A Dialogue with Nature: Nine Contemporary Sculptors.* Exhibition brochure. The Phillips Collection, Washington, D.C.,1992.

Kelly, Pam. "Piece at UNCC Is a Puzzle for Charlotte," *Charlotte Observer*, 20 May 1997, 1A.

Markoff, John. "CIA's Artistic Enigma Yields All But Final Clue," *New York Times*, 16 June 1999, A24.

McWilliams, Martha. "The Beautiful," *City Paper* (Washington, D.C.), September 1992.

Nesmith, Eleanor Lynn. "Natural Resources," *Washington Post Magazine*, 1 May 1994, 25.

"Peinliche Zwiebel," *Der Spiegel* (Germany), 27 May 1991, 239, 242.

Poole, Peter E., ed. *The Altered Landscape.* Reno and Las Vegas: Nevada Museum of Art in association with University of Nevada Press, 1999, 114–15.

Protzman, Ferdinand. "The Projection Artist's Otherworldly Landscapes," *Washington Post*, 25 March 1999, C1, C5.

Przybilla, Carrie. *Metaphysical Metaphors*. Exhibition brochure. High Museum of Art, Atlanta, 1994.

Ramo, Joshua Cooper. "C.I.A. Cryptic on Artwork," *Boston Globe*, 4 July 1990, 1, 20.

Richard, Paul. "Coded Creations, Inside Messages," *Washington Post*, 12 September 1992, G1, G4.

Rosenberger, Jack. "The CIA's Top-Secret Sculpture." *Art in America* (March 1991): 33.

Schwartz, John. "Sculpture's Code Tests Mettle of Cryptographers," *Washington Post*, 19 July 1999, A10.

Scott, Sue. *Secrets Passed*. Exhibition brochure. Orlando Museum of Art, Florida, 1993.

______. "Jim Sanborn: Covert Obsolescence, Secret Past." *Art Papers* (February 1993): 43.

Shannon, Joe. "Jim Sanborn at Numark." *Art in America* (October 1999): 172.

Shaw-Eagle, Joanna. "Artist Sheds New Light on Sculpture," *Washington Times*, 1 June 1997, D1, D4.

Sultan, Terrie. *Covert Obsolescence: Installations by Jim Sanborn*. Exhibition brochure. Corcoran Gallery of Art, Washington, D.C., 1992.

Tanguy, Sarah. "Jim Sanborn Studio Profile." *Sculpture* (January–February 1995): 16–17.

1980s

Allen, Jane Addams. "From the Realm of Aesthetics to the Arena of Life," *Washington Times*, 4 October 1984, B1.

______. "A Distant Viewing of Natural Settings," *Washington Times*, 13 January 1986, 1B, 3B.

Arnot, Denise. "Jim Sanborn." *New Art Examiner* (June 1982): 15.

Fleming, Lee. "Beyond Refinement." *Washington D.C. 1980* (Winter 1980–81): 84–87.

______. "Jim Sanborn at the Diane Brown Sculpture Space." *New Art Examiner* (March 1980).

______. "Washington's Museum Quality Artists." *Washingtonian Magazine* (October 1981): 57–68.

______. "Issues Are the Issue." *Art News* (January 1985): 84–89.

Forgey, Benjamin. "The Young Voices of Washington Sculpture," *Washington Star*, 15 October 1978, G4.

______. "Energy Emerges in Stone," *Washington Star*, 17 February 1980, E2.

______. "It Takes More than an Outdoor Site to Make Sculpture Public." *Art News* (September 1980): 84–89.

Fox, Howard N. *Rigging, Stacking, and Binding.* Exhibition brochure. Washington Project for the Arts, Washington, D.C., 1980.

______, Miranda McClintic, and Phyllis Rosenzweig. *Content: A Contemporary Focus*, 1974–1984. Exhibition catalogue. Hirshhorn Museum and Sculpture Garden, Smithsonian Institution, Washington, D.C.,1984, 143.

Freeman, Phyllis. *New Art*. New York: Harry N. Abrams, 1984, 166.

Freudenheim, Lewis M. *Baltimore's Public Art*. Exhibition brochure. Maryland Institute College of Art, Baltimore, 1980.

Henry, Gerrit. "Jim Sanborn." *Art News* (Summer 1985): 122–23.

Hess, Betsy. "The Art of the State," *Village Voice*, 16 February 1988, 39.

Hopps, Walter, and Eleanor Dickinson. *Atlantic Coast Pacific Coast*. Exhibition brochure. California College of Arts and Crafts, Oakland, 1982.

Jones, Carlton. "Outdoor Art for the Auto Age," *Baltimore Sun*, 14 August 1977.

Knight, Christopher. "Taking the Measure of U.S. Art and Artists," *Los Angeles Herald-Examiner*, 5 June 1988, E2.

Kuspit, Donald. *Awards in the Visual Arts.* Exhibition catalogue. Southeastern Center for Contemporary Art, Winston-Salem, N.C., 1988, 101–7.

Lewis, JoAnn. "With an Art of Stone," *Washington Post*, 2 February 1980, B5.

______. "At WPA, An Experimental and Ambitious Alternative," *Washington Post*, 12 July 1980, B7.

______. "Echoes of Nature's Power," *Washington Post*, 27 March 1982, C3.

Long, Glenn, and Nancy Beers. *Jim Sanborn Landscapes*. Exhibition brochure. Sunrise Museum, Charleston, W.Va., 1980.

Morgan, Robert C. "Jim Sanborn." *Arts Magazine* (Summer 1985): 18.

Richard, Paul. "'Content' Crammed," *Washington Post*, 4 October 1984, B1.

______. "The New Lay of Landscape," *Washington Post*, 11 January 1986, G1.

Rifkin, Ned. *Natural Settings.* Exhibition brochure. Corcoran Gallery of Art, Washington, D.C., 1986.

1970s

Freudenheim, Tom L., and James Melchert. *The 1978 Maryland Biennial.* Baltimore: Baltimore Museum of Art, 1978.

19th Area Exhibition. Exhibition brochure. Corcoran Gallery of Art, Washington, D.C., 1974.

Richard, Paul. "Scholarly Stories in Sculpture," *Washington Post*, 14 October 1978, B1.

21st Area Exhibition. Exhibition brochure. Corcoran Gallery of Art, Washington, D.C., 1978.

Virginia Artists 1973. Exhibition brochure. Virginia Museum of Fine Arts, Richmond, 1973.

Virginia Artists 1977. Exhibition brochure. Virginia Museum of Fine Arts, Richmond, 1977.

EXHIBITION CHECKLIST

All works are by Jim Sanborn. Courtesy the artist and Numark Gallery, Washington, D.C.

Critical Assembly, 1998–2003
Aluminum, brass, gold-, silver-, and nickel-plated brass, lead, stainless steel, boron-impregnated plastic, detector probes, Geiger-Muller (G-M) counters, simulated hydraulic lifts, graphite, wire, and sound
12 x 35 x 25', dimensions variable

The following works are all Ilfachrome prints, 30 x 36".

Albuquerque, N.M., July 16, 1945, 2001
Radium clock dial

Ancho, N.M., July 16, 1945, 2001
Radium clock dial

Carrizozo, N.M., July 16, 1945, 2002
Radium clock dial

Las Cruces, N.M., July 16, 1945, 2001
Radium clock dial

Polvadera, N.M., July 16, 1945, 2001
Radium clock dial

Gas Hills, Wyoming, 2001
Uranium autoradiograph

Joachimsthal, Bavaria, 2001
Uranium autoradiograph

Katanga, Congo, 2001
Uranium autoradiograph

Monticello, Utah, 2001
Uranium autoradiograph

Shinkolobwe, Congo, 2001
Uranium autoradiograph

PHOTOGRAPH CREDITS

Volker Dohne, fig. 33
Jan Faul, fig. 38
Mark Gulezian, Quicksilver, fig. 56
Hans Haacke, fig. 53
Hoachlander/Davis, figs. 42, 45, 46
Pete Mauney, fig. 5
Roman Mensing, fig. 54
Edwin N. York, fig. 1

ABOUT THE CONTRIBUTORS

Jonathan P. Binstock has been curator of contemporary art at the Corcoran Gallery of Art since January 2001. Among the many exhibitions he has organized are *Andy Warhol: Social Observer; Primary Properties: Mary Judge, Joseph Dumbacher John Dumbacher;* and *The 47th Corcoran Biennial: Fantasy Underfoot.* Reflecting his wide-ranging interest in art of the post-World War II era, he has written on artists as varied as Hung Liu, Bruce Nauman, Pepón Osorio, Mark Tansey, Wayne Thiebaud, and Alma Thomas. He is currently working on a retrospective exhibition of the paintings of Sam Gilliam.

Milena Kalinovska, an independent curator, was director of the Institute of Contemporary Art in Boston and associate curator of the New Museum of Contemporary Art in New York. She has organized numerous exhibitions, including *Boston School; The New Histories; William Christenberry: Changing Landscape—The Source Revisited;* and *Beyond Preconceptions: The Sixties Experiment.* She has published widely and is a contributor to *Trans Magazine* and is among the essayists in the collection *Words of Wisdom: A Curator's Vade Mecum on Contemporary Art*, published by Independent Curators International. She is also a consultant to *Primary Documents*, a sourcebook for eastern and central European art since the 1950s, published by The Museum of Modern Art, New York.

Barbara London, associate curator of video and media at The Museum of Modern Art, established the museum's video exhibition program and assembled its premier media collection. She has guided these programs over a long pioneering career. Her recent activities include Gary Hill's installation *HanD HearD; TimeStream,* a Web commission by Tony Oursler; and a series of Web projects undertaken in China, Russia, and Japan.

Howard Morland is the author of *The Secret that Exploded*, published by Random House, and "The H-Bomb Secret: To Know How Is to Ask Why," which appeared in the November 1979 issue of *The Progressive* magazine. Publication of the essay was delayed six months by a federal court injunction in a landmark application of national security "prior restraint" on print journalism. The injunction was unprecedented in duration but was rendered moot when the government dropped its case. He is a former Air Force pilot and congressional military policy analyst.

Jacquelyn Days Serwer is chief curator at the Corcoran Gallery of Art, where she oversees all museum activities. Her own work has focused on American and contemporary art. Most recently, she organized a retrospective exhibition of the work of Larry Rivers and contributed an essay to the accompanying book, *Larry Rivers, Art and the Artist*, published by Bulfinch Press.